Printmakers of the Baroque: 17th-Century Explorations of Space and Light

Featuring Artwork from the Collection of La Salle University Art Museum

Edited by
Susan M. Dixon

ISBN-10: 0988999935
ISBN-13: 978-0-9889999-3-0

Printmakers of the Baroque: 17th-Century Explorations of Space and Light

Essay Contributors: Rachel Christie, Susan M. Dixon, Megan Rankel, Klare Scarborough, Taylor Strickland

Label Contributors: Olivia Abney, Chikenye Akpunonu, Daniel Biester, Rachel Christie, Taylor Colaiacovo, Marlana Dalessandro, Susan Dixon, Sarah Finn, Elisabeth Giraud, Amanda Hershock, Amanda Martinez, Irene Martinez, Holly Michaels, Megan Rankel, Kelly Sheehan, Taylor Strickland, Emily Tomlin, Alonda White

Design Credit: Josh Ash

Photography Credits:

Photography of all catalogue illustrations provided by La Salle University Art Museum

Photo editing by Rebecca Oviedo

This book has been published with support from The Philadelphia Cultural Fund, The Pennsylvania Council on the Arts, and La Salle University Art Museum's Art Angels.

Book produced in conjunction with the exhibition:

Printmakers of the Baroque: 17th-Century Explorations of Space and Light, La Salle University Art Museum, Philadelphia, PA, December 16, 2013-February 28, 2014

ISBN-10: 0988999935

ISBN-13: 978-0-9889999-3-0

Printed by Lulu

Cover image: Abraham Bosse, *The Etcher and Engraver*, 1643, Etching.
Back cover image: Salvator Rosa, *Democritus in Meditation*, 1662, Etching and Drypoint.

Forword

European Baroque art of the 17th century is known for its dramatic explorations of space and light. Building on Renaissance developments in illusionism and single-point perspective, Baroque artists pushed the boundaries of visual representation, creating complex pictorial narratives that featured interesting vantage points, scenes within scenes, and striking light sources. In presenting images that were at once expansive, intimate and participatory, Baroque artists sought to engage their viewers in moralizing narratives, religious meditations, aesthetic appreciation, and social commentary.

Baroque artists also experimented with innovative printmaking techniques, particularly with the newly-developed medium of etching. Building on the popularity of engravings in the 15th and 16th century, 17th-century artists recognized the potential of printed images—which were inexpensive and easily transportable—to achieve widespread dissemination of their original compositions as well as reproductions of paintings by other master artists. Etching eventually came to supplant engraving as the preferred means of transferring artistic images onto paper during the 17th century because it allowed printmakers more versatility in creating pictorial effects. Baroque printmakers such as Jacques Callot experimented with etching techniques and materials, opening the way for master artists such as Rembrandt and Castiglione to create highly-detailed etchings with subtle shadings of light and dark.

The essays in this volume complement the recent exhibition of *Printmakers of the Baroque: 17th-Century Explorations of Space and Light* at La Salle University Art Museum during winter 2013-2014. Co-curated by La Salle Associate Professor of Art History Dr. Susan Dixon, the exhibition presented viewers with a fascinating display of Baroque virtuosity and experimentation. Featuring artists active in France, Italy, The Netherlands, and England, the exhibition illustrated the cultural diversity among printmakers, the range of representation and techniques, and the international exchanges that flavored 17th-century society. On display were prints which creatively depicted the non-European "Other" as well as people on the margins of society, such as peasants and soldiers returning from wars. The exhibition drew in La Salle community audiences as well as the general public, including adult groups, visiting pre-K-12 school groups and special needs groups. The exhibition also provided a foundation for a Baroque art history course at La Salle University taught by Dr. Dixon in spring 2014.

Dr. Dixon opens this catalogue with a provocative discussion about the diversity of Baroque printmakers. She gives an overview of the differences between printmakers who produced reproductive prints versus those who produced original compositions. She notes that the etching medium attracted artists who were interested in experimentation, including painters who sought to explore pictorial effects. Finally, she discusses artists and families of artists who specialized in printmaking, who were prolific and versatile in their production of images during the Baroque period.

Following this are essays by three undergraduate students enrolled in Dr. Dixon's Baroque art class in spring 2014. Taylor Strickland considers the reproductive printmaking of Orazio Borgianni and Pietro Aquila to address questions associated with authorship, ownership of design, and audience interpretation. Rachel Christie discusses the career of Giovanni Battista Castiglione and his development of innovative printmaking techniques such as the monotype etching process. Finally, Megan Rankel describes an important section in the gardens of French King Louis XIV in Versailles that was decorated with fountains and statues based on Aesop's Fables; now lost, the garden designs and their moral lessons were immortalized in the prints of Sebastien Le Clerc. Additionally, the catalogue includes artwork entries written by these and other students enrolled in the Baroque art history course, as well as by a few recent graduates of La Salle University.

Baroque printmakers produced a wealth of images, in both the quality and the quantity of artistic production. Their experimentation with technical processes placed them at the vanguard of innovation in the visual arts during the 17th century. Their production of images that depicted the everyday world around them, as well as extraordinary biblical stories and fables, had a strong appeal among contemporary 17th-century audiences— an appeal that continues to resonate among modern audiences today.

Klare Scarborough, Ph.D.
Director and Chief Curator
La Salle University Art Museum

Acknowledgements

The exhibition of *Printmakers of the Baroque: Explorations of Space and Light* was conceived at the suggestion of Art Museum Director and Chief Curator Klare Scarborough. It was staged in the winter of 2013, with the help of Curator of Art Carmen Vendelin and all the staff at the Art Museum. Because La Salle University's Department of Art History's mission is to engage the students with the Art Museum's collection in a variety of ways—and in this, it meshes with the Art Museum's mission—a project was hatched in which undergraduate students enrolled in the European Baroque Art class, in spring 2014, would help make exhibition wall labels for some prints.

Staging the exhibition was a collaborative effort, and I have many people to acknowledge for their help. Foremost, I express gratitude to Klare Scarborough for inviting me to co-curate the exhibition and for tossing out ideas on how to make it successful, both as a scholarly activity for myself, and more importantly, as a learning experience for La Salle students and for the University's art community. Carmen Vendelin gave me access to the collection and organized the logistics of the exhibition, arranging for the prints to be expertly framed and hung, and preparing the labels and wall texts for public display. With great patience, staff members Curator of Education Miranda Clark-Binder and Museum Assistant Rebecca Oviedo copyedited all of the exhibition text.

The students who participated in the spring 2014 Baroque Art course were eager to help with the exhibition. Because printmakers of the era are not often the most well-known of the Baroque artists (Caravaggio and Bernini, for example, never made prints), and because some of the printmakers are so little researched by scholars writing in English, La Salle undergraduate students were challenged as they compiled bibliographies and amassed information. Many of them rose to the occasion, and you will see their names and initials next to text they helped craft. These students are Olivia Abney, Kiki Akpunonu, Daniel Biester, Rachel Christie, Taylor Colaicovo, Marlana Dalessandro, Sarah Finn, Elisabeth Giraud, Amanda Hershock, Amanda Martinez, Megan Rankel, Tayor Strickland, Emily Tomlin and Alonda White. I especially thank Irene Martinez, an Art History major who was studying in Italy during the semester we were working on the exhibition, who graciously helped us out. Holly Michaels, a La Salle major in Nutrition, a student with a subtle understanding of how visual images work, also wrote labels for us. Three current Art History majors enrolled in the Baroque Art course, Taylor Strickland, Megan Rankel and Rachel Christie, wrote longer essays on issues highlighted by the exhibition, and I am very proud of them. Lastly, I thank Kelly Sheehan, a former Art History major and current graduate student in Education at La Salle University, who researched and wrote several labels. More significantly, Kelly also worked as my assistant, performing all kinds of fact-checking, organizing, and editing. Her attention to detail is much appreciated.

For the content of some parts of the exhibition, we relied on faculty colleagues at the University. Professor of Art History Mey-Yen Moriuchi helped us understand the chauvinism visible in a French 17th-century print of a defeated 16th-century Incan leader. Similarly, Professor of History Michael McInneshin steered us to bibliographic sources that helped us make sense of a print depicting people encountered by the Dutch in East Africa. Conversations with Chestnut Hill Professor of Art History Suzanne Conway also shaped our thinking about this print. Professor of Mathematics Steve Andrilli shared some ideas about the history of infinity, useful in grappling with a notion that had such meaning to 17th-century rulers, including King Louis XIV. Likewise, conversations with Sister Roseanne McDougall regarding the Catholic Reformation and images helped solidify some thinking in shaping the exhibition. Connelly Library's Special Collections Curator Sarah Seraphin was very gracious, as was Library Director John Baky, and they allowed us to display some of the illustrated books from the Susan Dunleavy Collection of Biblical Literature. These included a collection of miraculous stories associated with a painting in Florence

(Giovanni Angelo Lottini, *Scelti d'alcuni miracoli e grazie della Santissima Nunziata di Firenze* (Florence: Landini 1636), with prints by Jacques Callot); an emblem book based on the sayings of Horace (Otto van Veen, *Quinti Horatii Flacci emblemata* (Antwerp: Philip Lisaert, 1612), with printed illustrations by Gijsbert van Veen); and the polyglot *Book of Luke* from (*Quatuor evangelia arabice e latine* (Florence: Medici Press, 1591), with engravings by Antonio Tempesta). These books are gems in the extraordinarily deep jewel box of the Dunleavy Collection.

Professor of Art History Paul Crenshaw, from Providence College in Rhode Island, was the visiting guest speaker for the exhibition. Crenshaw is the author of *Rembrandt's Bankruptcy: The Artist, his Patrons, and the Art World in Seventeenth-Century Netherlands* (Cambridge: Cambridge University Press, 2006), among other scholarly writings on Rembrandt. His lively talk entitled "The Dutch Hustle" related Rembrandt's printmaking techniques and his relationship with his patrons. As intellectual as Rembrandt's imagery is, the Dutch artist's motives for printmaking were fame and financial gain. Crenshaw elaborated on how Rembrandt was not always the most honest or moral individual as he clamored for wealth.

I would be remiss if I did not express gratitude to the staff of Connelly Library for helping secure our research books through interlibrary loans. My students and I gave them plenty of work to do, and the staff did not flinch. The staff members at the Free Library of Philadelphia and at the Franklin Library of the University of Pennsylvania were equally amiable in locating bibliographic sources.

Throughout the catalogue, you will see the names of donors who have given the Art Museum prints over the years. I would like to especially thank James R. Tanis, the Director Emeritus of the Bryn Mawr College Libraries and Professor Emeritus of History, and his sons James T. Tanis and Justin Tanis, who donated prints to La Salle University Art Museum to enhance the exhibition. We were especially thrilled with a series of prints by Orazio Borgianni of scenes from Raphael's Loggia; a lovely print by the Flemish artist Gillis Neyts; a significant Claude Lorrain print, one of his Rape of Europa images; and my favorite, a little round print by Adriaen van Ostade representing activities performed by peasants in the winter months. Klare Scarborough also generously offered a print from her personal collection, one of Wencelaus Hollar's illustrations from John Ogilby's translation of Virgil's work. Without these thoughtful gifts and loans, the exhibition would have been less rich.

I express broad appreciation to all those researching and writing on the print culture of early modern Europe. The new information that is being discovered, and the formation of ideas about the nature of reproducible imagery and its markets in the 17th century, is exciting. I am grateful that my students and I had the opportunity to engage with this dynamic academic discourse this past year.

Lastly, thanks goes to the supporters and co-sponsors of the Baroque Print exhibition, related educational programs, and catalogue production include The Philadelphia Cultural Fund; the Pennsylvania Council on the Arts; the Brother Daniel Burke Endowment Fund for Education; La Salle University Art Museum's Art Angels; and La Salle University's Departments of Art History and Economics.

Contents

Foreword
Klare Scarborough, Ph.D.   5

Acknowledgements   7

List of Catalogue Illustrations   11

List of Figure Illustrations   13

Printmakers of the Baroque
Susan M. Dixon, Ph.D.   15

'After Raphael': Thoughts on Reproductive Printmaking of the 17th Century
Taylor Strickland, La Salle University Class of 2014   19

Castiglione: Italian Baroque Printmaker Extraordinaire
Rachel Christie, La Salle University Class of 2015   23

Illustration 1   27

Aesop's Fables and the Gardens of Versailles in Le Clerc's Prints
Megan Rankel, La Salle University Class of 2015   29

Illustrations 2-6   33

Bibliography   39

Appendix A: Catalogue of Artworks   45

History of La Salle University Art Museum   90

List of Catalogue Illustrations

Cat. 1, Abraham Bosse, *The Etcher and the Engraver*, 1643, 10 1/8" x 12 1/2", 81-G-1119

Cat. 2, Lieven Cruyl, *View of St. John Lateran, Rome*, c. 1664-66, 14 3/4" x 18 3/4", 76-G-613

Cat. 3, Claude Lorrain, *The Roman Forum*, 1636, 7 7/8" x 10 3/8", 07-G-3410

Cat. 4, Israël Silvestre, *Port de Conférence*, c. 1660s, 2 1/2" x 5 7/16", 77-G-767

Cat. 5, Gabriel, Nicolas, and Adam Perelle, *The Grand Water Basin*, late 17th century, 7 7/8" x 10 3/8", 13-G-3551

Cat. 6, Sébastien Le Clerc, Illustrations from *Aesop's Fables*, 1683, 2 3/16" x 1 3/4" each, 85-G-1341 (Selections from 1-23)

Cat. 7, Wenceslaus Hollar, *On the North Side of London*, 1665, 3 7/8" x 2 1/2", 77-G-758

Cat. 8, Gillis Neyts, *Man and His Dog*, 17th century, 5 3/16" x 6 1/4", 13-G-3584, Gift of James T. Tanis and Dr. Justin Tanis

Cat. 9, Claude Lorrain, *Coast Scene with Rape of Europa*, 1634, 7 7/8" x 10 3/8", 13-G-3585, Gift of James T. Tanis and Dr. Justin Tanis

Cat. 10, Pierre Lombart, after Anthony Van Dyck, *Henry Frederick Howard, the 22nd Earl of Arundel*, 1652, 13 5/8" x 10 3/8", 14-G-3658

Cat. 11, Jacques Callot, Illustrations from *Capricci di varie figure*, 1617 or 1623, 2 1/4" x 3 1/8" each, 13-G-3586, Gift of James T. Tanis and Dr. Justin Tanis

Cat. 12, Rembrandt van Rijn, *Beggar Man and Woman Conversing*, 1630, 2 5/8" x 2", 96-G-3200, Gift of Mr. and Mrs. Jay Stiefel

Cat. 13, Adriaen van Ostade, *The Empty Jug*, c. 1653, 4" x 3 3/8", 81-G-1133

Cat. 14, Adriaen van Ostade, *The Pig Killers*, c. 1642, 4 3/4" diameter, 13-G-3583, Gift of James T. Tanis and Dr. Justin Tanis

Cat. 15, Cornelis Bloemaert II, after Abraham Bloemart, *A Hunter Resting by a Tree*, c. 1626, 4 3/16" x 6", 90-G-3071

Cat. 16, Giovanni Benedetto Castiglione, *Head of a Man with a Moustache, Wearing a Fur Headdress, Facing Left*, mid- to late 1640s, 5 5/8" x 4 9/16", 82-G-1211

Cat. 17, Jan van Doetechum, the Younger, after Jan Huygen van Lindschoten, *Christian and Muslim Couple from Mozambique*, 1596, 10 3/8" x 8 3/16", 96-G-3199, Gift of Mr. and Mrs. Jay Stiefel

Cat. 18, Jérôme David (attributed), after Claude Vignon, *Atahualpa, Incan Emperor*, 1635, 8 3/4" x 7 1/4", 13-G-3550

Cat. 19, Jan Georg van Vliet, after Rembrandt van Rijn, *Laughing Man in a Gorget*, c. 1634, 10 9/16" x 8 3/8", 70-G-296

Cat. 20, Rembrandt van Rijn, *Self-Portrait with Raised Saber*, 1634, 4 13/16" x 4", 76-G-596

Cat. 21, Claude Mellan, *The Sudarium*, or *The Veil of St. Veronica*, 1649, 16 7/8" x 12 3/8", 69-G-257

Cat. 22, Simone Cantarini, *Adam and Eve*, 1639, 7 3/4" x 6 7/8", 79-G-1031

Cat. 23, Stefano della Bella, *Flight into Egypt*, 1652, 5 13/16" x 4 13/16", 70-G-295

Cat. 24, Stefano della Bella, *Virgin and Child with St. John*, 1641, 5 7/8" x 4 13/16", 73-G-445

Cat. 25, Jacques Callot, *Judith with the Head of Holofernes*, c. 1630, 3 15/16" x 2 11/16", 76-B-1(g)5

Cat. 26, Jusepe de Ribera, *The Drunken Silenus*, 1628, 10 11/16" x 14", 77-G-746

Cat. 27, Hendrick Goudt, after Adam Elsheimer, *Tobias and the Angel*, 1613, 10 1/8" x 10 9/16", 77-G-776

Cat. 28, Jan van de Velde II, after Moses van Uyttenbroeck, *The Angel Departing from Tobit and Tobias*, c. 1630, 5 3/16" x 6 1/4", 80-G-1079(4)

Cat. 29, Ferdinand Bol, *Holy Family in an Interior*, 1643, 7 $\frac{1}{8}$" x 8 $\frac{3}{8}$", 75-G-530

Cat. 30, Jeremias Falck, after School of Raphael, *Virgin and Child with St. Anne*, c. 1655-58, 15 $\frac{3}{4}$" x 11 $\frac{9}{16}$", 02-G-3268

Cat. 31, Wenceslaus Hollar, after Francis Cleyn, *Women at Work*, c. 1654, 11 $\frac{11}{16}$" x 7 $\frac{7}{8}$", 13-G-3552, Gift of Dr. Klare Scarborough

Cat. 32, Rembrandt van Rijn, *Presentation in the Temple*, c. 1640, 11 $\frac{1}{2}$" x 8 $\frac{1}{2}$", 72-G-352

Cat. 33, Rembrandt van Rijn, *Supper at Emmaus (larger plate)*, 1654, 6 $\frac{1}{2}$" x 5", 82-G-1222, Gift of Dr. and Mrs. William K. Sherwin

Cat. 34, Rembrandt van Rijn, *Descent from the Cross by Torchlight*, 1654, 5" x 6 $\frac{1}{2}$", 76-G-587

Cat. 35, Giovanni Benedetto Castiglione, *Finding of the Bodies of Sts. Peter and Paul*, 1647-50, 11 $\frac{13}{16}$" x 8 $\frac{1}{16}$", 81-G-1173

Cat. 36, Sébastien Bourdon, *Giving Water to the Thirsty*, 1666-71, 17 $\frac{1}{8}$" x 23", 74-G-500

Cat. 37, Orazio Borgianni, after Raphael, *Moses and the Burning Bush*, 1615, 6 $\frac{1}{4}$" x 7 $\frac{3}{16}$", 13-G-3587

Cat. 38, Pietro Aquila, after Raphael, *The Triumph of King David*, 1674, 10" x 11 $\frac{3}{8}$", 81-G-1167

Cat. 39, Salvator Rosa, *Democritus in Meditation*, 1662, 14 $\frac{1}{2}$" x 8 $\frac{1}{2}$", 68-G-239

Cat. 40, Salvator Rosa, *The Academy of Plato*, c. 1662, 18" x 10 $\frac{7}{8}$", 68-G-238

List of Figure Illustrations

Fig. 1, Rembrandt van Rijn, *The Second Oriental Head*, c. 1635, 5 $^7/_8$" x 4 $^{15}/_{16}$", etching, 1933-72-1514, William S. Piling Collection, Philadelphia Museum of Art

Fig. 2, Sébastien Le Clerc, *Plan of the Labyrinth*, from *Le Labyrinthe de Versailles* (Paris, 1679), unnumbered page, engraving, 717 L112, Franklin Library, University of Pennsylvania Libraries

Fig. 3, Sébastien Le Clerc, *Entry to the Labyrinth*, from *Le Labyrinthe de Versailles* (Paris, 1679), unnumbered page, engraving, 717 L112, Franklin Library, University of Pennsylvania Libraries

Fig. 4, Sébastien Le Clerc, *Fountain of the Wolf and the Crane*, from *Le Labyrinthe de Versailles* (Paris, 1679), page 43, engraving, 717 L112, Franklin Library, University of Pennsylvania Libraries

Fig. 5, Sébastien Le Clerc, *Fountain of the Fox and the Stork*, from *Le Labyrinthe de Versailles* (Paris, 1679), page 29, engraving, 717 L112, Franklin Library, University of Pennsylvania Libraries

Fig. 6, Sébastien Le Clerc, *Fountain of the Foxes and the Grapes*, from *Le Labyrinthe de Versailles* (Paris, 1679), page 57, engraving, 717 L112, Franklin Library, University of Pennsylvania Libraries

Printmakers of the Baroque

The breadth of print production of the European Baroque period, echoed in the breadth of the print holdings of the age in the La Salle University Art Museum, demands some consideration. The prints attest to the various ways printmakers engaged with the evolving profession in the century. A growing body of collectors among the aristocratic and the bourgeois classes of 17th-century Europe fueled an increased demand for engravings and etchings, both in number and in variety of subject, and artists catered to that demand.[1] The newly developing medium of etching, often said to be a process that replicated the art of drawing and that sidestepped the requirement of strenuous manual labor needed for engraving, attracted printmakers trained in painting.[2] The makers of Baroque prints were a sundry lot, then, as some came from the trade profession of metalworking, while others came from the ranks of court painters and art academicians. The exhibition held in winter of 2013-14 illustrated the diversity of these printmakers, their motivations and their techniques, as they explored Baroque notions of space and light in their prints.

The Art Museum's holdings include the work of reproductive printmakers, those who copied the designs of other artists' paintings or sculptures. The beginnings of such printmaking activity are associated with Marcantonio Raimondi (c. 1480-c. 1534) who copied Raphael's frescoes, at the behest of that artist.[3] The result was to make the master's work more widely known, and hence more famous, the aspiration of many Renaissance artists. By the 17th century, reproductive printmakers were working with permission of the artists or of the works' owners. Jeremias Falck was one of a handful of engravers who provided a print gallery, or paper museum, of the Dutch Reynst Brothers' collections of paintings [cat. 30]. Similarly, famous collectors such as Marchese Vincenzo Giustiniani in Rome and Sir Thomas Howard, Earl of Arundel, in London also hired numerous printmakers, including Claude Mellan and Wencelaus Hollar, to immortalize the art, antiquities, and other objects in their possession.[4] Some printmakers focused their energies on reproducing the work of one painter, as in the case of Hendrick Goudt and Adam Elsheimer [cat. 27]. Some painters, including Sébastien Bourdon, reproduced their own paintings in order to secure greater audiences for their imagery [cat. 36]. At sustained moments in their careers, Claude Lorrain and Salvator Rosa would do the same, with the intent to make their more successful paintings well known [cat. 3, 39].

Furthermore, publishers and print sellers coordinated projects for reproductive printmakers.[5] They distributed tasks among various types of artists, contracting with printmakers to engrave or etch metal plates using drawings supplied by others. Sometimes the printed imagery was conceived as a series, such as the ever popular character heads, known as tronies in Northern Europe, mimicking the portrait heads of ancestral kings or rulers [cat. 16, 18 19]. They were sometimes bound, and sometimes not, so that the seller could impress individual prints depending on buyers' demands. Publishers' control over making impressions also could be the case with views of cities on the Grand Tour [cat. 2], and in illustrated literary works such as the translations of classical texts by John Ogilby [cat. 31].

In all parts of Europe, engravers tended to come from families of printmakers in which one generation passed on the skills of working directly in metal, and the expensive presses and other equipment needed to create prints. Prints signed with the name Perelle often cause confusion among connoisseurs because it is difficult to distinguish between the hands of different family members [cat. 5]. Although there are no women printmakers represented in the exhibition, there were some active in this age. Given the communal nature of making prints and the restrictions placed on the movements of 17th-century women, most all were taught by family members, as in the case of Diana Scultori and Elisabetta Sirani.[6] Etching, however, as a process that requires the artist to mark out the design in a sticky ground rather than to cut it directly into the metal plate, attracted those who wanted to experiment with the medium, among them a number of painters.

Some 17th-century printmakers were primarily painters, and they used etching to experiment with pictorial effects. These artists tended to create original compositions of their own design. Rembrandt and Giovanni Benedetto Castiglione are good examples of the painter-printmaker [cat. 33, 34, 35].[7] In their quest for pictorial excellence, they attempted to replicate the effects achieved in painting, especially in regard to light and shadow, in etching. Thus they often devised new methods of digging or inking the plates. Furthermore, by making prints that sold to a wider market, they found some independence from the patronage system in which they ceded the choice of subject matter, among other things, to another.[8] In that sense, printmaking allowed for modern ideas about art-making to take root. In addition, both Rembrandt and Castiglione used the medium to cater to the growing market. Rembrandt was the most aggressive and successful in this manner. Late in his career, he found ways to make each of his reproducible prints exceptional, by altering the plates frequently, using different papers, and limiting the number of copies pulled from a plate [cat. 34, 35].

Rembrandt and Castiglione were exceptional in the period. Many painters did printmaking only occasionally, most often returning to paint as their primary medium. Claude Lorrain executed prints for only a few years of his life and abandoned making them completely by mid-career [cat. 9]. Jusepe de Ribera, as well, picked up the medium for some years, only to return to painting, but not before making some exquisite prints, such as the *Drunken Silenus* [cat. 26]. Gillis Neyts, the highly prolific landscape painter and draftsman of the Mosan Valley region, made relatively few prints [cat. 8]. Salvator Rosa took up printmaking in two distinct periods in his life, in the 1620s and again in the 1660s. Unlike Rembrandt and Castiglione, these artists usually are not credited with adding anything innovative to the etching process. Most did it with new markets in mind. Rosa, in particular, aspired to gain some financial and intellectual independence from patrons by making prints [cat. 39, 40].

Lastly, there were the Baroque artists who only worked in print media. Jacques Callot and Stefano della Bella are the most noted examples. These artists are often credited with transforming the etching process in innovative ways by inventing new tools, biting acids or grounds, or promoting new ways of making lines and shadows. They produced all types of subjects for varied commissions and projects, including scenes of recent and past events – theatrical events, weddings, funerals, battles—religious images and playing cards [cat. 11, 23, 24, 25]. Other dedicated printmakers specialized in one subject. Viewmakers created highly saleable prints of famous sites. The well-travelled Israël Silvestre produced over 1,000 prints of various European cities [cat 4]. The Perelle family specialized in French palaces and gardens, including Versailles [cat. 5]. Some of these printmakers traveled long distances to record their views. Born in Bohemia (modern-day Czech Republic), Wenceslaus Hollar produced highly marketable views of London [cat. 7] while the Flemish Lieven Cruyl captured views of Rome [cat. 2]. Of these two, Hollar was incredibly versatile in his output, producing numerous prints in every subject category, while Cruyl abandoned the activity after making 23 prints in Rome.

In 17th-century France, attempts to include printmaking among the fine arts, with the same status as painting and sculpture which required training of the intellect as well as the hand, made headway in a manner not achieved in Italy or the Netherlands. The argument that etching had much in common with drawing, however, was not useful in that campaign. Engraving was popular in the court of France for a longer period than elsewhere in Europe before it became an obsolete process by the end of the century. Abraham Bosse argued for the dignity of printmaking, and he was the first printmaker to be elected to the Royal Academy of Fine Arts [cat. 1]. Others followed. From 1661 forward, Louis XIV named various printmakers as his royal engravers, among them Sébastien Le Clerc and Claude Mellan [cat. 6, 21].

The diversity of the 17th-century printmakers' approaches to printmaking accounts for the broad array of the prints' subjects and the artistic interpretations of those subjects, and for the richness of styles and techniques. The La Salle University Art Museum's collection provided ample evidence of the Baroque printmakers' talents.

Susan M. Dixon, Ph.D.
Associate Professor of Art History
Chair, Fine Arts Department
La Salle University

1   William W. Robinson, "'This Passion for Prints': Collecting and Connoisseurship in Northern Europe during the Seventeenth Century," in *Printmaking in the Age of Rembrandt*, ed. Clifford S. Ackley (Boston: Museum of Fine Arts, 1981), xxvii-xlviii; and Sue Welsh Reed and Richard Wallace, *Italian Etchers of the Renaissance and the Baroque* (Boston: Museum of Fine Arts, 1989), xvi-xvii.

2   This position is nuanced in Michael Cole and Larry Silver, "Fluid Boundaries: Formations of the Painter-Etcher," in *The Early Modern Painter-Etcher*, ed. Michael Cole (University Park: Pennsylvania State University Press, 2006), 4-35.

3   Lisa Pon, *Raphael, Dürer, and Marcantonio Raimondi: copying and the Italian Renaissance Print* (New Haven: Yale University Press, 2004).

4   Luigi Ficacci, *Claude Mellan, gli anni romani. Un incisore tra Vouet e Bernini* (Rome: Multigrafica Editrice, 1989), 101-116, 294-316; and Richard Pennington, *A Descriptive Catalogue of the Etched Work of Wenceslaus Hollar 1607-1677* (Cambridge: Cambridge University Press, 1982), xxii-xxvi.

5   See Reed and Wallace, *Italian Etchers*, xvi; Paolo Bellini, "Stampatori e mercanti di stampe in Italia nei secoli XVI e XVII," *I quaderni del conoscitore di stampe* 26 (1975), 19-34; and Nadine Orenstein, "Marketing prints to the Dutch Republic: Novelty and the print publisher," *Journal of Medieval and Early Modern Studies* 23 (winter 1983), 141-165.

6   See Adelina Modesti, *Elisabetta Sirani: Una Virtuosa del Seicento Bolognese* (Bologna: Editrice Compositori, 2004); Gioconda Albricci, "Prints by Diana Scultori," *Print Collector* 12 (1975), 17-23, 51-57; Stefania Massari, *Incisori Mantovani del '500: Giovan Battista, Adamo, Diana Scultori e Giorgio Ghisi dalle collezioni del Gabinetto Nazionale delle Stampe e della Calcografia Nazionale* (Rome: De Luca Editore, 1981); and Lia Markey, "The Female Printmaker and the Culture of the Reproductive Print Workshop," in *Paper Museums: The Reproductive Print in Europe 1500-1800*, eds. Rebecca Zorach and Elizabeth Rodini (Chicago: University of Chicago Press, 2005), 51-75.

7   Cole and Silver, "Fluid Boundaries," 21-23.

8   Francesca Consagra, "The Marketing of Pietro Testa's 'Poetic Inventions'," in *Pietro Testa, 1612-1650: Prints and Drawings*, ed. Elizabeth Cropper (Philadelphia: Philadelphia Museum of Art, 1988), lxxxvii-ci.

'After Raphael': Thoughts on Reproductive Printmaking of the 17th Century

By the 17th century, reproductive printmaking was an established practice of copying original paintings, sculptures, and sometimes drawings and prints. In particular, reproductions of works by Italian Renaissance masters such as Michelangelo and Raphael were in high demand throughout Europe. Reproductive printmakers were a specific cohort of printmakers who undertook this task. This essay will consider the work of two such printmakers, Orazio Borgianni (1565-1616) and Pietro Aquila (1630-1692) in an effort to raise, if not fully answer, certain issues associated with the activity. How was a reproductive print regarded in relationship to the original work? Did issues such as ownership of the design come into play? The fact that some artists were more talented than others, or had particular stylistic preferences, must have affected their visual interpretation of the original design. Was this recognized in 17th-century Europe?

Reproductive prints helped master artists gain fame for their work because prints—given the large number of impressions that can be pulled from a plate and the transportability of the sheets—helped increase knowledge of original works of art and thus the fame of the artists. Prints were used to outfit the personal home, purchased in great numbers by individual collectors, and employed as visual teaching aids in art studios and academies. In general, prints substituted for original works when individuals could not travel to see the original artworks. Reproductive prints were the precursors of photography, and sometimes still serve today as alternatives to photography. They also serve as historic memorials of lost or unpublished works of art. They have aided those who study art history in many ways. Art historian David Alexander noted that some "prints of a painting made before restorers and other 'improvers' laid their hands on it can be very revealing."[1]

The issue of ownership of the image is one that we today are absorbed by, but it was one that did not exist in this period. We are concerned with copyright of an image, or permissions to publish a reproduction of an image. At the heart of this is a keen respect for originality and ownership of a design or idea. Contemporary artists are protected by a number of laws. The Creative Common Licence (2001), for example, allows creators of original content to give reproduction rights to other individuals, companies, and artists. This transfer of rights, however, requires that credit be given to the original artist or author, and there are usually some stipulations. It reflects relatively new notions that did not exist in the 16th and 17th centuries. Reproductive printmakers often worked for the master artist, or sometimes for the owner of the original work of art, but there seemed to be no law that restricted the reproductive printmaker from copying whichever original design he/she chose. That said, market demands made certain works more profitable to copy than others. As stated above, the Italian masters' works were much admired and demanded. In many cases, a system of identifying the engraver or etchers as distinct from the original artists (and later, the publisher) emerged. Some prints acknowledge the original thought behind the composition or subject.[2] In particular, the use of "invenit" in the signature line indicates "the person in whose mind the image arose."[3] Other terms were also used. The terms "fecit"and "sculpit" ("made" and "engraved," respectively) sometimes appear with the name of the original artist while "inc." ("incised") appears after the name of the reproductive printmaker.

Another issue raised by reproductive prints was that of accuracy. Reproductive printmakers were not necessarily creating exact replicas of the original works of art. Instead, the market for such prints produced a situation in which there was a large variety of visual interpretations of the original work.

Print connoisseurship was an emerging field of study in the 17th century. And there was some concern about the authenticity of prints, i.e., that they were by the hand of one engraver or etcher or another.[4] Illegal copying of prints in 16th and 17th centuries in Europe was "widespread, explicit, and well documented."[5] However, creating reproductions of paintings and sculpture was a long established tradition and was not subject to the same kind of scrutiny.[6]

Art historian Linda Hults noted, "Reproductive prints after the Italian Renaissance Masters… were placed in the first category (Masters whose works are esteemed above all others) along with superb original prints."[7] The work of Raphael and Michelangelo above all were incredibly popular among collectors. The frescoed imagery of Raphael and Michelangelo was in especially high demand. Alexander argued that their work "assumed a status as artistic sources equal to nature and antiquity."[8] They fueled the market for reproductive prints in Italy, the Netherlands, and France. Workshops in the Netherlands such as that of Hieronymous Cock churned out hundreds of these reproductive prints for a wide variety of audiences and distributed them en masse.[9] Flemish artists were even trained in an Italian style in order to provide accurate reproductions.[10]

With this information, we can examine the two images in the La Salle University Art Museum exhibition. They were both created after frescoes by Raphael, and both, incidentally, were etched by Italian painters who also made prints. The first print is Orazio Borgianni's *Moses and the Burning Bush* [cat. 37], produced in 1615. It represents one of Raphael's 52 scenes on the frescoed ceilings of a Loggia in the Vatican Palace. Borgianni reproduced all of the scenes, which were bound together without a titlepage and sold as a set. The second is Pietro Aquila's *The Triumph of King David* [cat. 38], part of another series of prints by various printmakers based on Raphael's frescoes, which were bound together in *Imagines Veteris ac Novi Testamenti a Raphaele Sanctio Urbinate in Vaticani Palatti* (*Images of the Old and New Testament in the Vatican Palace by Raphael Sanzio from Urbino*), and published in 1674. In the analysis of these prints, the accuracy of the etched copy of the original will be assessed. If prints were disseminated to many people, then one would expect them to be as close to the original design as possible. Instead, the works' accuracy was not criticized by their 17th-century owners.

Moses and the Burning Bush depicts the moment in which God calls Moses over to the bush in order to proclaim him the savior of the Israelites. In *Exodus 3*, God proclaims the land that Moses is standing on as sacred. Moses, in fright, kneels on the ground and covers his face in awe of God.

Borgianni loosely interprets Raphael's style. He was more concerned with capturing the overall composition and the individual forms in the composition in order to convey the narrative. For prints after history paintings, this was a common way to approach the practice: "the meaning and composition were much more important to the engraver than the original details of the form."[11]

Borgianni's print is small in comparison to Aquila's, and the quality of the line is sketchy. These etched lines are unable to capture the sense of texture in the leafy trees or the burning bush. They cannot capture the luminescence and reflective quality of the water or sky in the background. In regards to line compensating for the lack of color, Borgianni falls flat in this reproduction.

The Triumph of King David was one of four scenes in the Loggia which tell the story of David and his trials and successes. The scene depicts David as king after defeating the Philistines and the Arameans. According to the Old Testament, he confiscated enough to pull 100 chariots filled with stolen gold, and he turned the Arameans of Damascus into servants (2 *Samuel* 8). David rides in one of these chariots, surrounded by his triumphant army carrying booty. In the foreground is a captive who has been disarmed and dismounted. His posture is slumped and his arms are chained behind his back.

Aquila's reproduction maintains its accuracy and honesty. The image is very similar to Raphael's original in terms of composition and detail, and is lacking only in color. Scholars have noted that the engraver's line can imitate and correct for the absence of color.[12] The illusion of color in Aquila's black-and-white print is suggested through the richness of tone achieved by his etched lines.

Raphael's fresco is difficult to see with any clarity because of its location on the ceiling. It also may have been restricted to viewers during the 17th century because it was part of the private papal apartments. Aquila's details – the muscular horses, the look in the horses' eyes, the various expressions of the triumphant soldiers and the prisoner, etc. – must have been appreciated in the print.

Aquila gives us a good sense of atmospheric perspective (which is used to some degree in the original), as well as the shading, by employing crosshatching and stippling techniques. His shading captures a wide variety of tones that move swiftly from dark to light, tones that Raphael had created with color. Overall, if prints are supposed to serve as accurate and academic examples, this print is successful in that endeavor.

What is missing from *The Triumph of King David* as well as *Moses and the Burning Bush* is a tribute or credit to Raphael as the originator of the compositions. Aquila acknowledges his own involvement when he inscribed "Petrus Aquila del. e sculp.", meaning he drew the image and cut the plate. Raphael is credited in the inscription "R.V.I in Vat", meaning Raphael of Urbino invented this image, which is in the Vatican. Borgianni's print *Moses and the Burning Bush* does not credit Raphael as the originator of the design at all. The print does not have an explanatory inscription at the bottom of the image as in Aquila's. The artist's signature, "HB", for Horatio Borgianni, is found with the date 1615 in the leftmost corner on a rock.

These slights to Raphael—and Borgianni's is greater than Aquila's—provoke some questions. Did the buyers/collectors know they were getting reproductive prints? Was identifying Raphael as the original creator necessary? Were the images so famous that sophisticated print sellers and buyers did not need to be informed the original images were by Raphael? Were Borgianni and Aquila being dishonest in some way by omitting or obscuring Raphael's name? It might not be possible to know the answers. One thing is for certain, that printmakers such as Borgianni and Aquila did not have to deal with various copyright laws. Rebecca Zorach, author of *Paper Museums*, describes the era as "the Age of Imitation, when artistic education became codified as a practice of copying the highly prized works of the past."[13]

Taylor Strickland
La Salle University Class of 2014

1   David Alexander, "'After-Images': A Review of Recent Studies of Reproductive Print-Making," *Oxford Art Journal* 6, no. 1 (1983): 11.

2   Ibid., 42.

3   Ibid., 52.

4   Abraham Bosse, *Sentiments sur la distinction des diverses manières de peinture, dessein, & gravure, et des originaux d'avec leurs copies* (Paris: chez Bosse, 1649) informed collectors how to distinguish an original print from a copy.

5   Lisa Pon, "Prints and Privileges: Regulating the Image in 16th Century Italy," *Harvard University Art Museums Bulletin* 6, no. 2 (1998): 42.

6   Ibid., 48.

7   Linda C. Hults, *The Print in the Western World: An Introductory History* (Madison: University of Wisconsin Press, 1996), 257.

8   Hults, *The Print in the Western World*, 257.

9   Alexander, "'After Images'," 12.

10 Timothy A. Riggs and Larry Silver, *Graven Images: the Rise of Professional Printmakers in Antwerp and Haarlem* (Evanston, IL: Northwestern University Press, 1993), 3.

11 Alexander, "'After Images'," 15.

12 Hults, *The Print in the Western World*, 264.

13 Rebecca Zorach and Elizabeth Rodini, eds., *Paper Museums: The Reproductive Print in Europe 1500-1800* (Chicago: University of Chicago Press, 2005), 3.

Castiglione: Italian Baroque Printmaker Extraordinaire

It is said that few artists of Giovanni Benedetto Castiglione's day understood and exploited the artistic possibilities that the medium of etching had to offer.[1] Castiglione's etchings were highly valued among his fellow etchers and among 17th-century collectors. This essay recounts his career as an artist, and elaborates on his distinctive style of etching. Furthermore, it acknowledges what many scholars believe to be his significant technical innovation in printmaking, the invention of the monotype print.

Castiglione was born in Genoa, Italy, in March 1609. The eastern Mediterranean port city was an economic and cultural hub of exchange for dominant European enterprises. The city's elite, who had attained great wealth through trade and banking, had an appetite for collecting works of art to decorate their homes and chapels, and to build their private collections. Castiglione's ongoing study of work by established artists created an environment favorable to his development as an artist.[2]

We know something of Castiglione's training and career from contemporary biographers. Several state that Castiglione studied under multiple artists as a youth.[3] However, because there are inconsistencies in the biographies, it is difficult to decipher the exact time frame in which he trained under different instructors, including second-rate artists like Giovanni Battista Paggi and Giovanni Andrea de Ferrari. We know, however, that these artists seem to have only a minimal amount of influence on his later artistic production. At first, Castiglione was well known for his depictions of animals and pastoral scenes.[4] Only over time did his subject matter include more prestigious religious and mythological subjects, which required command of the human figure. His early style was more Mannerist than Baroque, with its attenuated figures, unnatural lighting and contrived compositions. But Castiglione was an ambitious artist, intent on fame and fortune. His style as well as his subject matter would change after he left Genoa at the age of 20. In addition, by his mid-30s and through his 40s he would embrace the new medium of etching to help achieve his goals.

What the biographers are consistent about is that Castiglione's personality was not that of a gentile courtier artist. In his early adulthood, he had a reputation for violent behavior.[5] For instance, Castiglione fired a weapon at a fellow artist after a dispute. He was accused of all types of sadistic behavior against family members. Later in life, he destroyed his own works in front of a patron, in a whirlwind of fury and anger. Despite his bad temperament, Castiglione aspired to be and eventually positioned himself as one of the most sought-after artists of his generation.

A credit for his success is given to his extensive travels as a young artist. Castiglione bid his native Genoa farewell and traveled to Rome in 1630, returning occasionally for commissions, but never for long. He was once referred to as "a constant, irrepressible traveler."[6] Through the course of his life, Castiglione ventured to all Italy's court cities, including Naples, Venice, Mantua, Florence, Parma, Bologna and many other cities with thriving artistic centers. While travelling, Castiglione immersed himself in the art found in each of the cities. In doing so, he exposed himself to a greater array of styles as well as techniques. He was "an insatiable magpie" in that respect.[7] In the 1630s, Castiglione made tremendous strides in fostering his own style, known for its Baroque naturalism but also for its "painterly bravura."[8] Thus it can be said that Castiglione was more influenced by the art he saw—Caravaggio, Annibale Carracci, Guido Reni, Peter Paul Rubens, and Nicolas Poussin—rather than what he studied in Genoa.[9] However, as Castiglione developed and matured as an artist, he became fascinated with the works of Rembrandt, which he saw in prints.[10] As a result, they made a lasting impression on Castiglione's subject matter as well as his artistic style. But it was not only Rembrandt's art that attracted Castiglione. He admired the Dutch artist's fame and financial success, and he aspired to emulate Rembrandt to attain the same.

His absorption of Rembrandt's aesthetic is most apparent in his etchings. As someone who embraced different artistic media with ease, Castiglione created the majority of his etchings in the mid- to late 1640s, while in Rome. He focused primarily on Rembrandt's etchings of a series of *Heads* made in the 1640s.[11]. During this period, the Dutch were fascinated by people from other parts of the world, as well as exotic animals and goods. As a result, they frequently sought out prints which captured these things as a sort of entertainment. Rembrandt's *Heads* would not be considered portraits; they were character heads or "tronies," made as a kind of tongue-in-cheek imitation of the popular portrait heads of ancestral kings and heroes. Castiglione, like many other printmakers, created a series of heads and entered into a flourishing market for them. For Castiglione, the prints showcased his ability to be inventive and to compose rich dramatic compositions which tapped into a deeper range of psychological, cultural and physical types. Because these prints could be sold internationally, he hoped they would ensure his fame.

Rembrandt, already considered a master artist by the 1640s, produced some of the most sought-after prints on the market. Castiglione was one of the first Italians to acknowledge and refer to Rembrandt's work. To make the point about Castiglione's reliance on the Dutch master, it is useful to compare Rembrandt's *Second Oriental Head*, c. 1633-36 [fig. 1] with Castiglione's *Man with a Mustache and a Fur Headdress* [cat. 16].[12]

Rembrandt's *Oriental Head* portrays an elderly man, seen in profile, with unkempt whiskers and mustache. His profile is distinct, with a long misshapen nose and deep-set eyes. He wears an elaborate headdress of wool bound by a woven cloth, and a tattered fur jacket with a frilly white scarf or cravat. He casts his eyes downward. He seems neither engaged nor animated. Instead, the print portrays the man's psychology as contemplative and remorseful to some degree. His age is seen in the sagging of his shoulders, the wrinkles on his brow. Rembrandt filled the piece with rich texture, using short

and varied energetic lines. Rembrandt was known for creating exquisite shadowing, and he does so here, to the man's back. A hint of a shadow climbs the back wall.

When this print is compared to Castiglione's *Man with a Mustache and a Fur Headdress*, even an untrained eye could see the similarities between the two images. Like Rembrandt's figure, Castiglione's old man with the shaggy beard and mustache faces toward the left. Likewise, his shoulders appear slumped forward and his head hangs down ever so slightly. The downward glance of his deep-set eyes indicates a state of contemplation and resignation. The man's costume is not dissimilar from that of Rembrandt's old man, with the unusual hat and garments.

Castiglione's handling of the etching needle is different from that of Rembrandt. While Rembrandt used the needle economically, Castiglione's lines show great energy. With light flicks of the needle, the Italian artist was able to capture the wrinkles, especially those around the eyes, before they dissipate into the shadows of the face. He also rendered a wide array of textures, including hair, fur, feathers, and fabric. Castiglione was able to create such illusions by utilizing crosshatching, stipple, flicks and dashes of the etching needle. The fur of the cap is created by curved lines, swooping forward and up along the brim of the hat. The feather is created through light detailing and careful attention to marking. The individual tails of the feathers curve together at the old man's shoulder and are visible along the edges where they flare out ever so slightly. Castiglione used precise, very lightly-etched lines to create texture in the bunched fabric on the old man's collar. The man's facial hair is drafted much the same as the fur on his cap. Castiglione used outward sweeping lines and crosshatching to shade the old man's scruffy beard and to build the shadow lining the perimeter of his face.

By emulating artists like Rembrandt, Castiglione mastered a technique known as "tenebrism," or the dramatic use of light and dark in a figural composition. In *Man with a Mustache and a Fur Headdress*, a dark shadow sweeps from the left side of the image towards the figure at its center. The shadow then absorbs part of the figure's chest and shoulder. In this way, Castiglione underscores the mood of the old man. Compared to Rembrandt's *Oriental Head*, the shadow in Castiglione's *Man* is more evident and intense.

As his career progressed, Castiglione's reputation grew and his wealth began to accumulate. Like some printmakers of his generation, including Rembrandt, Pietro Testa and Salvator Rosa, Castiglione wished to be free of the market system—working through publishers and print sellers – and to create prints that rivaled painting in their scholarly and inventive subject matter. Castiglione knew that such prints would be attractive to elite collectors both in and visiting Rome.[13] He succeeded, and by the late 1640s, Castiglione was producing a dynamic range of complex subjects, derived from classical and religious sources, in his distinctive style. They include *Diogenes Searching for an Honest Man*, *Circe with the Companions of Odysseus Transformed into Animals*, and *Tobit Burying the Dead*.

Among this group of prints, in the mid- to late 1640s, Castiglione created *Finding the Bodies of Sts. Peter and Paul*.[14] It depicts a legend describing how circa 300-400 C.E., a group of men stumbling through the ancient Roman catacombs, the underground burial places, found the incorrupt bodies of the two figurehead saints of the Catholic Church. The figure closest to the viewer in the foreground is the beheaded St. Paul. Behind his body lies St. Peter, holding the keys which were given him by Christ as a symbol of his role as the institutional leader of the Church. Peter represented the legitimacy of the Catholic Church and served as a symbol of its continued strength in the 17th century.

The significance of the image derives from the religious disputes of the Baroque era. Following the Protestant Reformation and Catholic Counter Reformation, tensions were high as each religious group sought to reclaim the believers for its own. Peter had been rejected by the Protestants in favor of Paul. Here Paul is re-appropriated, placed by the side of Peter, equal in their martyred fates and in their role in the early history of the Church shared by Protestant and Catholic alike.

The etching also showcases Castiglione's aptitude for conveying luminosity through high-contrast tenebrism. In this image, the men cling to one another as the torch casts light upon the corpses. The torch light serves a dual purpose. First, it provides a sense of depth and perspective. The light reflects and casts itself along the walls of the cavernous space, allowing the viewer to grasp the size of the perceived space within the catacomb. Castiglione was able to carry the illumination of the torch throughout the space. The light seems to creep up the walls, creating shadows in the crevices and highlighting the more craggy areas of the stone. At the same time, the light falls upon the foreground of the image. In doing so, Castiglione dramatized the men's faces as they gape upon the two recumbent bodies of the saints.

As in *Man with a Mustache and a Fur Headdress*, Castiglione utilized the full range of etching techniques to create the desired textures and shadows. Examine, for instance, the folds and shadows of Sts. Peter and Paul's robes. Castiglione used simple lines to define the figures and loose crosshatching to create the shadows. In addition, he used an overlapping stippling and flicking technique to create the texture of the stone walls. Castiglione took advantage of the options offered by etching. Rather than relying on consistent outlines, he exploited the density of the curved lines to create the illusion of organic shapes.

Invention of the Monotype

Castiglione was a curious and innovative artist, and is often credited with improving upon the etching process and inventing monotype etching. [15] Etchings were created by drawing on the surface of a metal plate, often copper or zinc, with a needle or a burin. The tool would cut directly into an acid-resistant resin, rather than into the plate itself, as it would in the engraving process. Once the design was completed, the plate would be submerged in an acid bath. At this point in the process, the acid would bite into the sections of the plate which were no longer protected by the resin. The longer the sections were subjected to the acid bath, the darker the lines would appear in the final print. Once pulled from the bath, an artist would remove the resin, warm the plate, apply ink, gently place printing paper atop the plate, and run it through a press. The print thus emerged.

As Castiglione's work took on a more fluid painterly style, he developed another method of etching that prefigured the monotype print process. Unlike traditional etchings, monotypes require applying a mixture of oil and coarsely ground pigment onto a plate's surface, and lightly cutting a design into that mixture using a brush.[16] The mixture can be manipulated to create different effects in the print. The more pigment was added to the oil, the more opaque the lines would appear. If less pigment was added to the oil, the lines would appear more transparent in the print.[17]

Castiglione's monotype process offered a unique set of characteristics. It allowed for the creation of fluid and dynamic networks of lines. Because the artist used brushes rather than needles or burins, he could create a painterly expressiveness with the movement of each stroke. Monotypes also facilitated the creation of sophisticated tenebristic effects. Because the contrast between lights and darks was a function of the amount of pigment added to the oil, Castiglione no longer needed to revisit and modify the plates, or to carefully apply thick layers of printer's ink to the plates, in order to create darker lines.

Not everyone is convinced that Castiglione's prints executed with this process can be classified as the first monotypes. Nonetheless, they illustrate his inventiveness and his ongoing search for a means to distinguish himself as a Baroque printmaker.

Rachel Christie
La Salle University Class of 2015

1   Timothy Standring and Martin Clayton, *Castiglione: Lost Genius* (London: Royal Collection Trust, 2013), 12.

2   Ibid., 17.

3   Ibid., 17-23.

4   Ibid., 26-30.

5   Ibid., 11.

6   Anthony Blunt, "The Drawings of Giovanni Benedetto Castiglione," *Journal of the Warburg and Courtauld Institutes* 8 (1945): 161.

7   Standring and Clayton, *Castiglione*, 12.

8   Ibid., 54.

9   Ibid., 25-26. In Naples, he was influenced by Jusepe de Ribera. Ibid., 37.

10 Ibid., 43.

11 Ibid., 81.

12 Most of Castiglione's *Heads* date from the mid- to late 1640s. This one is dated to 1650-52 based on style.

13 Standring and Clayton, *Castiglione*, 57-78.

14 Ibid., 73.

15 Anthony Blunt, "The Inventor of Soft-Ground Etching: Giovanni Benedetto Castiglione," *Burlington Magazine* 113, no. 821 (1971): 472; and Sue Welsh Reed, "Giovanni Benedetto Castiglione's 'God Creating Adam': The First Masterpiece in the Monotype Medium," *Art Institute of Chicago Museum Studies* 17, no. 1 (1991): 66-73, 94-95.

16 Standring and Clayton, *Castiglione*, 79-81.

17 Ibid.

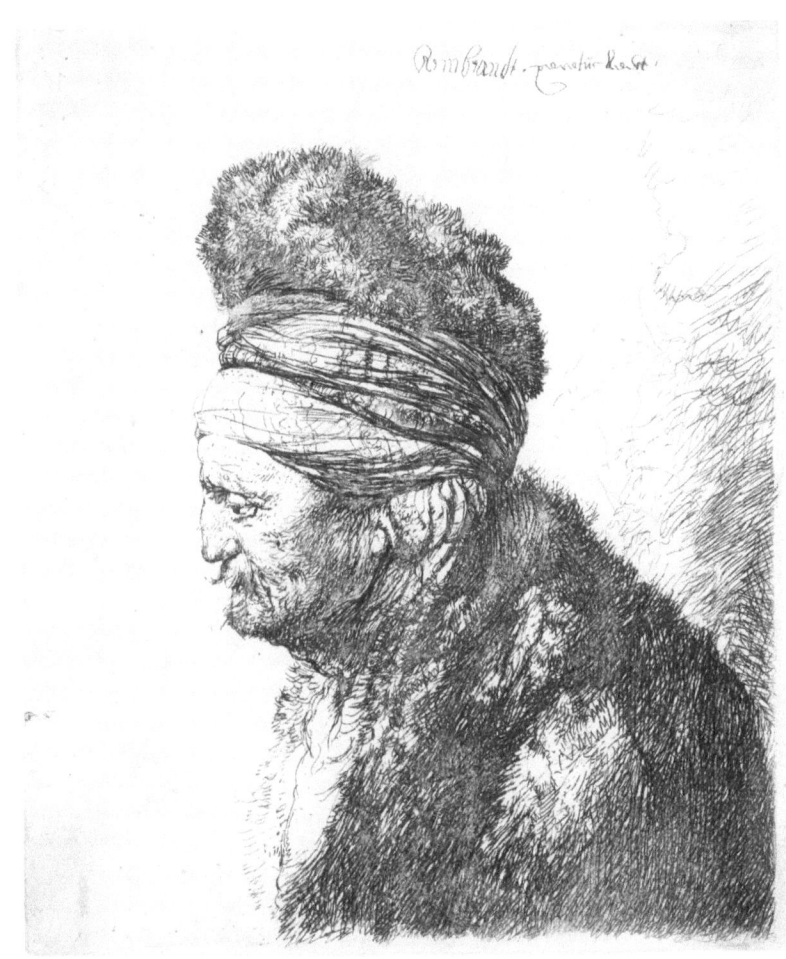

Fig. 1, Rembrandt van Rijn
The Second Oriental Head, c. 1635
5 7/8" x 4 15/16", etching
1933-72-1514
William S. Piling Collection, Philadelphia Museum of Art

Aesop's Fables and the Gardens of Versailles in Le Clerc's Prints

Sébastien Le Clerc, the royal printmaker to French King Louis XIV, engraved a set of 22 small oval prints illustrating some of *Aesop's Fables*. The majority of the prints represent scenes of talking animals from the famous fables. The set was printed without text in 1683. Le Clerc dedicated them to the King's very powerful Controller General of Finance, and the unofficial Minister of Culture, Jean-Baptiste Colbert, who was an avid print collector.[1] The set was one of a series of small prints that Le Clerc created for Colbert and other high society French print collectors. Other sets were of architectural views, of ancient Greek and Roman philosophers, and of the costumes of various French royal subjects. However, this series of *Aesop's Fables* was unusual in that the illustrations resembled some of the most popular fountains in a section of the newly opened gardens at Louis XIV's palace at Versailles. Le Clerc also engraved rectangular images of the fountains, which were published in a guidebook of the Labyrinth, the part of the gardens in which the fountains were placed. The illustrated guidebook written by Charles Perrault was originally published in 1677, and it underwent many re-issues and translations.[2] This essay will focus on three of Le Clerc's rectangular engravings of the fountains, which share subjects and compositional elements with three of the oval prints from Aesop's Fables. They are *The Wolf and the Crane*, *The Fox and the Stork*, and *The Fox and the Grapes*. The two sets of prints attest to the popularity of the fables in French society in the reign of Louis XIV, from 1666 to 1715.

Aesop was a Greek slave and storyteller who lived from around 620-560 B.C.E. His stories were used to teach moral lessons of the time. Many of the lessons are universal and timeless. By the 15th century, his fables were put down in writing, and fables by other authors were added to them. By the 17th century in Europe, *Aesop's Fables* had been translated into many languages and published many times.[3]

Charles Perrault was an author at the court of Louis XIV. He was intrigued by the fables, and in emulation of them, he instituted a new literary genre called the fairy tale. His tales included well-known stories such as *Sleeping Beauty* and *Puss and Boots*.[4] Perrault was also a French civil servant charged with supervising the King's buildings. He held this office during the early stages of the renovation and construction of the palace and gardens at Versailles. In the early 1670s, Perrault convinced Louis XIV that the fables would serve as good subject matter for garden ornaments, in particular for fountains. Perrault felt that the fountains would teach important lessons to the 10-year old Dauphin, or prince, while at the same time entertaining him.

Perrault masterminded the design of the Labyrinth, although the design was executed by André Le Notre, the king's gardener.[5] It was a leafy maze, of high boxwood, with winding pathways leading to a central destination, and some 39 clearings at the intersection of the pathways [fig. 2]. Each of the 39 clearings held a fountain illustrating one of *Aesop's Fables*. The Labyrinth and its fountains were begun in 1672 and completed in 1677. Unfortunately, in 1778 King Louis XVI had the fountains and the plantings removed. But in the late 17th century, they attracted many from the royal court and beyond. Perrault wrote the abovementioned guidebook for this part of the garden.

As can be seen in one of Le Clerc's guidebook illustrations, there were two statues flanking the entranceway to the Labyrinth [fig. 3]. One was of the elderly Aesop. The scroll in his hand identifies him as the author of the 39 fables on display inside. The second statue was of Cupid, the god of Love. He holds a ball of silken thread between his fingers.[6] The two figures were there to lead and support the visitors metaphorically as they made their way through the maze. Aesop created the lessons, but Cupid provided the means for the visitor to navigate successfully through the lessons without getting lost. The one figure was old, grotesque and wise, and the other was young, beautiful and often mischievous. Both oversaw the visitors' experience of the Labyrinth.

This section of the garden was made for a purpose, according to Perrault.

"The lesson of instruction to be drawn from this fiction is this: That tho' the God of Love is too apt to involve mankind into a thousand petty broils and perplexities, yet he has the secret art of extricating them out of the maze they are thus led into, when he is accompanied by *Prudence*, to the practice whereof he is here directed by the sage Fables of Aesop."[7]

Once inside the maze, the visitors navigated the pathways and came upon the clearings. There they would see visions of the lively animals acting out the narratives of the fables in front of them. In total, 333 statues of animals decorated the 39 fountains in the Labyrinth. The statues were made of brass and were painted naturalistically to make them seem more real.[8] To further the illusion, the statues were posed in lively ways to replicate the action of the animals in the fables. The marble basins, decorated with shells, represented appropriate settings for the fables. For example, there was a sculpted grape arbor in the fountain for *The Fox and the Grapes* [fig. 6; cat. 6(16)], and a central pedestal for the leader mouse in a round basin encircled with mice in *The Council of the Mice*.[9] The layout of the maze ensured that no matter where visitors were standing they could see at least three fountains.[10]

A large copperplate accompanied each fountain. On it was inscribed a poem written by the poet Isaac de Benferade. The poems explained the fable and its lesson.[11] The young Dauphin learned to read while absorbing valuable life lessons from the copperplates. Many visitors flocked to the Labyrinth for amusement as well as education.

This paper will now consider three of Le Clerc's rectangular prints of the fountains and the correspondent oval illustrations in the series of prints for Colbert. The first print is of the *Fountain of the Wolf and the Crane* [fig. 4]. These two figures are located in the middle of a flat round basin. The crane is standing, its stalk legs

apart, and its long neck is curved over in the direction of the wolf. Its beak nearly reaches the wolf's mouth. The wolf is sitting on its hind quarters. His head is tilted backward, and his mouth is open. A tall column of water shoots up from his mouth. Beneath the two animals are some bones, the remains of a supper the wolf had just consumed. The bones appear more prominently in the oval print [cat. 6(17)]. The crane's bill is more deeply inserted into the wolf's mouth in the smaller print than it is in the guidebook print.[12]

The story relates that the wolf was choking on a bone from a meal he had just finished. The crane passed by, and the wolf convinced the crane to help remove the bone from his throat. The wolf promised a sum of money for the deed. Once the crane had removed the bone, the crane asked for his payment. The wolf merely replied that the crane should be grateful for being able to leave with his head still attached to his body, because the wolf could have easily eaten the crane.[13]

This fable conveys a very important lesson to the gardens' visitors. The lesson is that in serving the powerful and the dangerous, in this case represented by the wolf, one should not expect a reward. Rather, one should be grateful to escape without injury. Another moral was that the greedy, as represented by the crane, should not expect gratitude.

LeClerc's illustration of *Fountain of the Fox and the Stork* depicts the two animals on opposite sides of a central elevated platform in a round basin [fig. 5]. The fox places its forelegs on the elevated basin while its hind legs remain in the lower. His head is back as if in mid-howl, and water shoots from his mouth. The stork is perched on the lip of the elevated basin. Her neck is gracefully bent over, and her long bill is deep inside a narrow jar which is set in the center of the elevated basin.[14] In Le Clerc's small oval print, the fox stares intently at the stork, and the jar's shape is slightly different, with a narrow neck on a spherical base [cat. 6(2)].

The fountain represents the second half of a narrative about the fox and the stork. According to Aesop, the fox was jealous of the stork's elegance and wanted to make her look silly. He invited her over for dinner. The fox served up a thin broth in a shallow bowl. The stork, of course, was unable to drink the broth because her long bill would not allow it. She politely thanked the fox, and she left hungry. The next night, she invited him to dinner. She served him broth in a tall glass jar. The stork could easily drink from the jar, but the fox, with his short snout, could not. He was angry, and he yelled at her. The stork replied that she expected the fox to enjoy his dinner as much as she had enjoyed the dinner he served her.[15]

The lesson here is to not play tricks on your neighbors if you cannot stand the same treatment. In other words, this is the Golden Rule: "Do unto others as you would have done to you." This was an important lesson for the success of civic society in late 17th-century France, as it is today.

The third fountain illustration is the *Fountain of the Fox and the Grapes* [fig. 6]. Along the back perimeter of a nearly rectangular basin sits an arbor made of three arched bays and covered in grape vines. A tiered fountain sits in the middle of the basin. The grape clusters on the vines are out of reach of the two foxes, who are standing on their hind legs, on either side of the basin. Water shoots from the foxes' mouths, representing their frustration at being unable to eat the grapes. It also shoots from the several places in the arbor, as if the grapes are taunting the animals.[16] The small oval print replicates only the right half of the fountain's composition, wherein one fox clambers after the grapes dangling from one-and-a-half bay of arbor [cat. 6(16)].

The story is that a hungry fox saw grapes hanging high off the ground. After many failed attempts to get them, the fox eventually gave up. He was exhausted and angry. As he walked away, he muttered that they were sour grapes and certainly not good enough for him to eat.[17]

The moral of this story is that when something does not go as planned and people do not get what they want, people act as if they never wanted it anyway, and that the goal was not worthy of their efforts. This moral was essential for the young prince, because as he grew up, the Dauphin always received what they wanted. However, there would be a day when he would not. The fable would teach him to be mature and accept defeat. Perrault picked this fountain for that reason.

The success of Perrault's idea was more than anyone could have imagined. The young Dauphin loved the Labyrinth and the lessons that he learned there, but the French court and its visiting diplomats loved it as well. All diplomats were given a tour of the gardens, particularly of the *Aesop's Fables* fountains. This explains the popularity of Perrault's guidebook and its many re-issues and translations.[18] Visitors could take home a reminder of what they had seen in the gardens of Versailles. The rectangular illustrations of the fountains are some of Le Clerc's most circulated prints. Their popularity might help us understand why Le Clerc made the small oval prints for Minister Colbert, who surely would have appreciated them. There are far fewer impressions of these oval prints than the guidebook illustrations, so they are rarer and thus more valued. Also, without the restrictions of having to conform to a fountain design, Le Clerc made Aesop's talking animals more lively.

Megan Rankel
La Salle University Class of 2015

1   *Oeuvres choisies de Sébastien Le Clerc, chevalier romain, dessinateur et graveur du cabinet du roi, contenant 239 estampes, dessinées et gravées par ce célèbre artiste, représentant des costumes, des fables, des paysages, et autres objets intéressant* (Paris: chez Lamy, 1784), 24, fig. 96-118.

2   Charles Perrault, *Le Labyrinthe de Versailles*, originally published 1677, reprint with preface by Michel Conan (Paris: Editions du Monteur, 1981). Perrault first published Isaac de Berserade's poems and a description of the gardens in 1672, and then issued the edition with Le Clerc's illustrations in 1677.

3   The first 17th-century French translation was by Jean Baudoin, *Fables d'Ésope Phrygien* (Paris: chez Matthieu Guillemot, 1631), and it was reissued many times throughout the century.

4   Philip Neil and Nicoletta Simborowski, *The Complete Fairy Tales of Charles Perrault* (Boston: Houghton Mifflin Harcourt, 1993). Some of his other fairy tales are *Little Red Riding Hood*, *Bluebeard*, and *Cinderella*.

5   Michel Baridon, *A History of the Garden of Versailles*, trans. Adrienne Mason (Philadelphia: University of Pennsylvania Press, 2008), 130.

6   Perrault, *Le Labyrinthe*, 3 and 6-7; and W.H. Matthew, *Mazes and Labyrinths*, (London: Dover, 1970), 55.

7   David Bellamy, *Ethic Amusements* (London: W. Faden, 1796), 210. The words are Perrault's, translated by Bellamy. Bellamy's book was one (although not the first) of the English-language translations of Perrault's guidebook.

8   Perrault, *Le Labyrinthe*, 4-6.

9   Ibid., 24, 50-51.

10   Guy Walton, *Louis XIV's Versailles*, (Chicago: University Chicago Press, 1986), 30.

11   Perrault, *Le Labryinthe*, 2-79.

12   Ibid., 21, 42-43.

13   Aesop, *The Complete Fables*, trans. and ed. Olivia Temple and Robert K. G. Temple (New York: Penguin Books, 1998), 167.

14   Perrault, *Le Labyrinthe*, 16, 28-29.

15   Jerry Pinkney, *Aesop's Fables* (New York: SeaStar Books, 2000), 46. This fable is not included in Aesop, *The Complete Fables*, and therefore is considered one of the fables that was added to the collection after Aesop's death.

16   Perrault, *Le Labyrinthe*, 26, 56-57.

17   Aesop, *The Complete Fables*, 27.

18   Baridon, *A History of the Garden of Versailles*, 121.

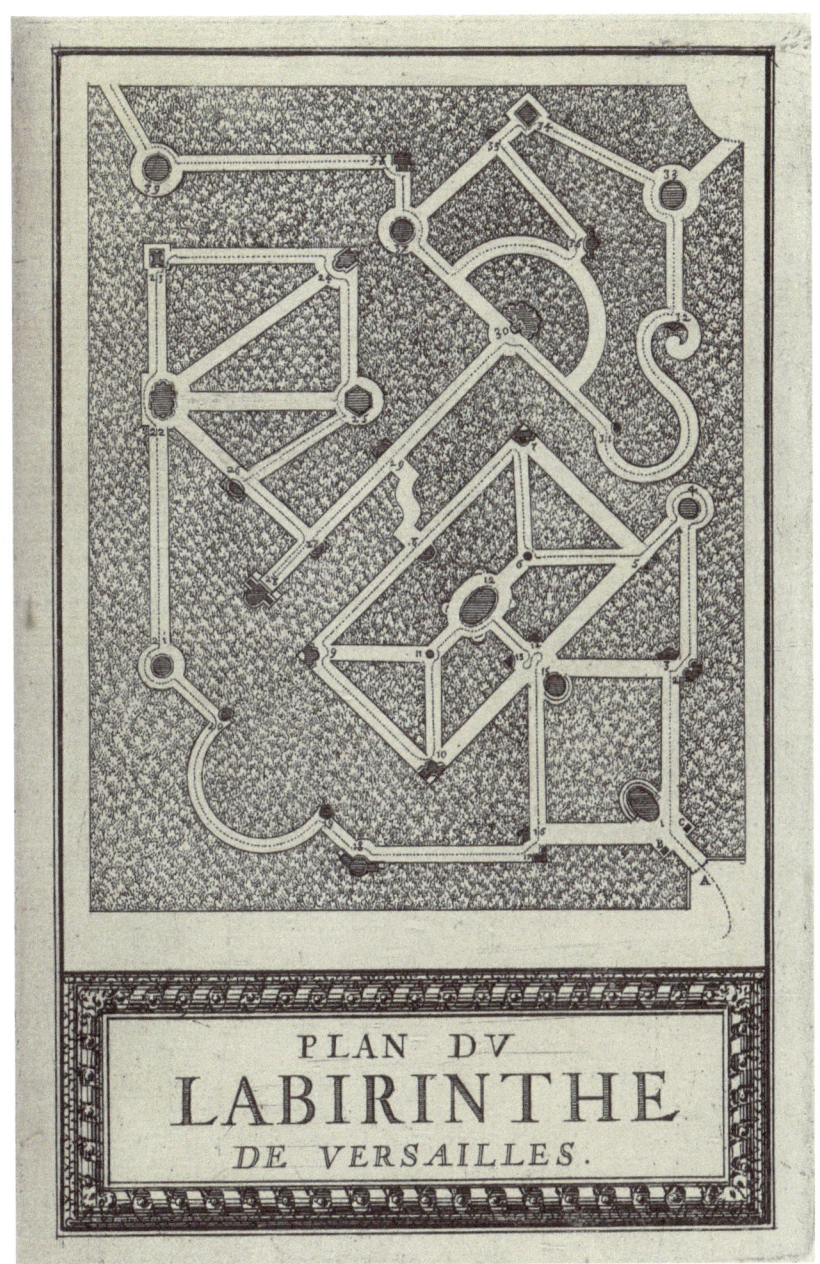

Fig. 2
Sébastien Le Clerc
Plan of the Labyrinth, from *Le Labyrinthe de Versailles* (Paris, 1679), unnumbered page
engraving
717 L112
Franklin Library, University of Pennsylvania Libraries

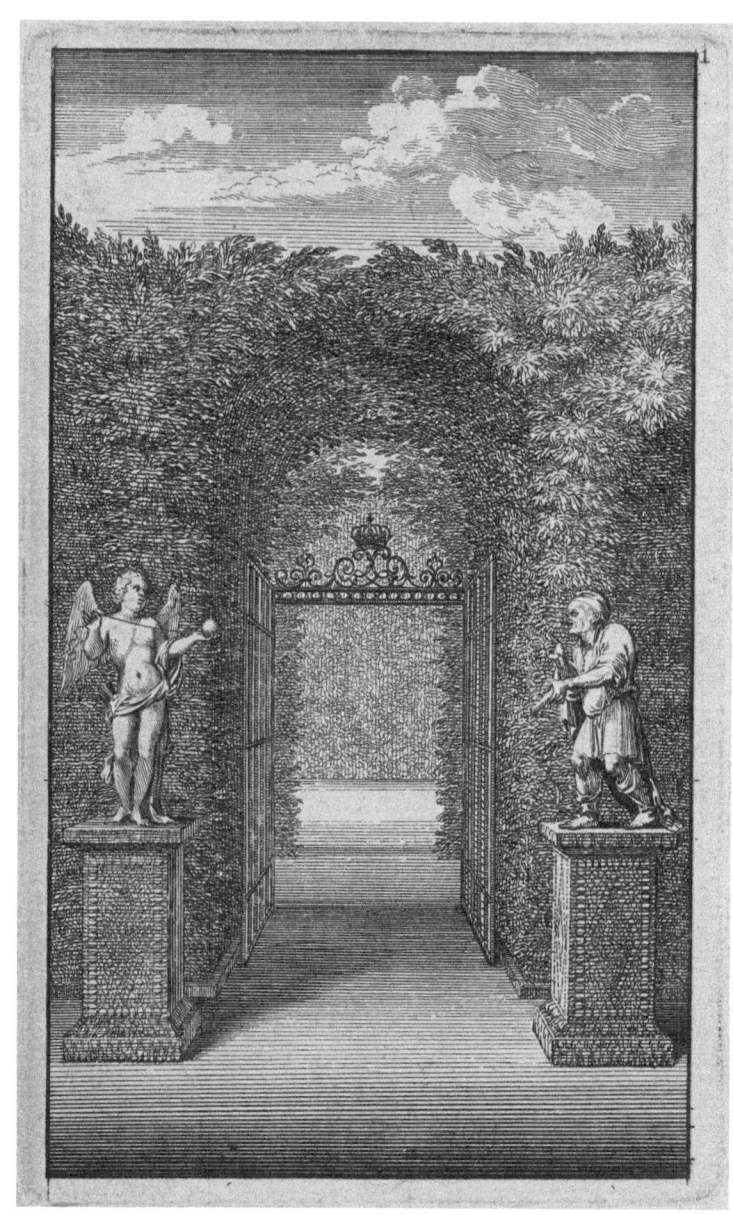

Fig. 3
Sébastien Le Clerc
Entry to the Labyrinth, from *Le Labyrinthe de Versailles* (Paris, 1679),
unnumbered page
engraving
717 L112
Franklin Library, University of Pennsylvania Libraries

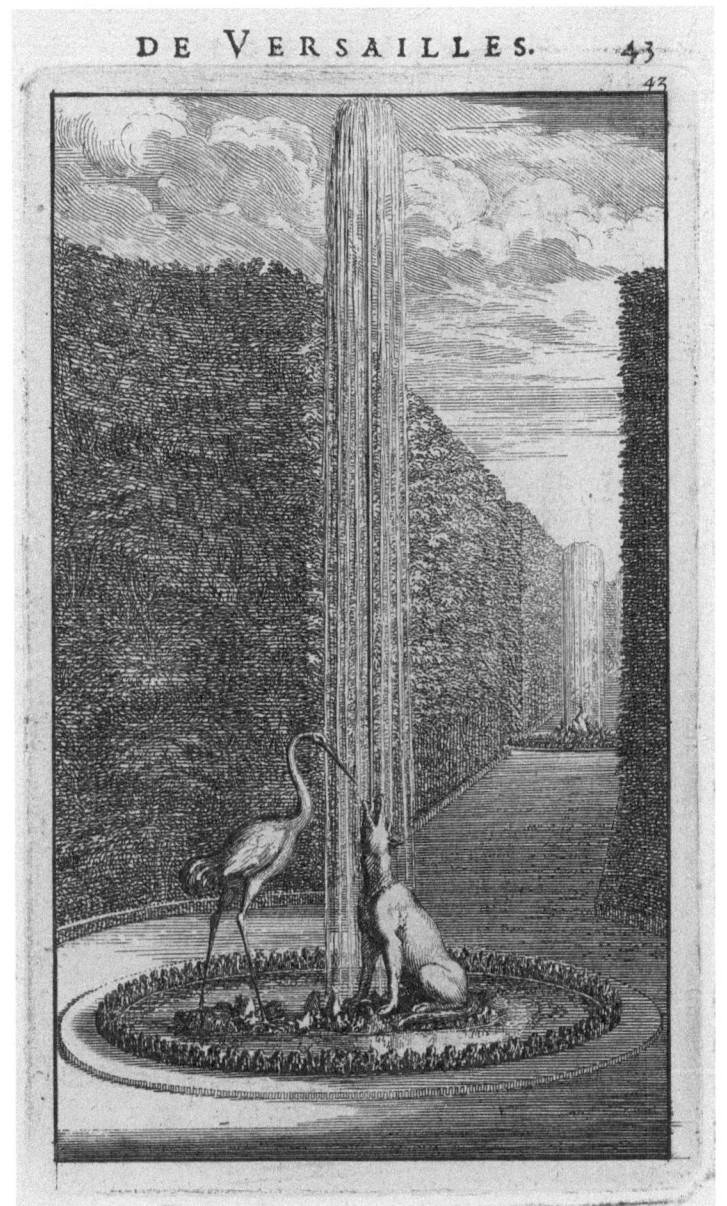

Fig. 4
Sébastien Le Clerc
Fountain of the Wolf and the Crane, from *Le Labyrinthe de Versailles* (Paris, 1679), page 43
engraving
717 L112
Franklin Library, University of Pennsylvania Libraries

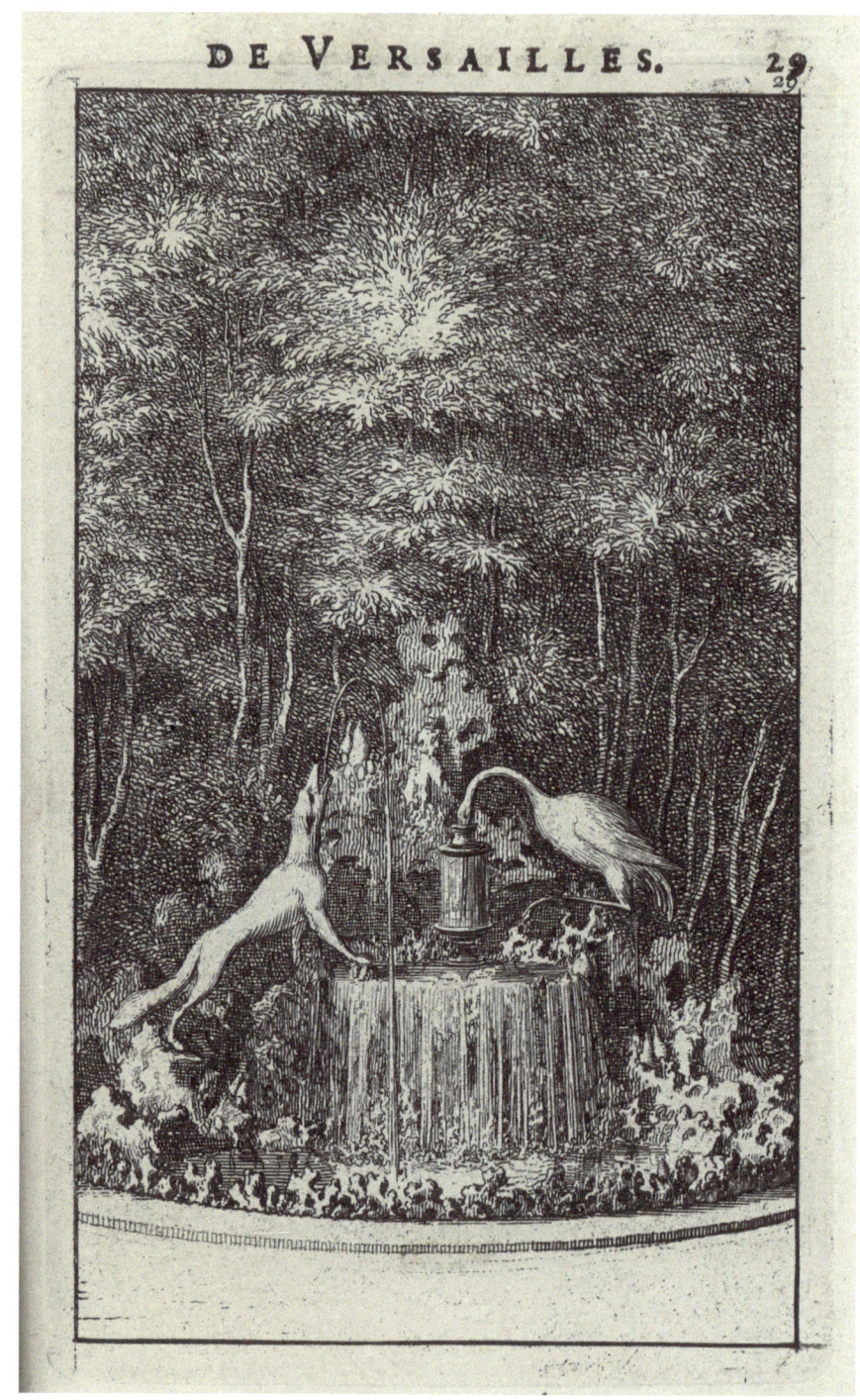

Fig. 5
Sébastien Le Clerc
Fountain of the Fox and the Stork, from *Le Labyrinthe de Versailles* (Paris, 1679), page 29,
engraving
717 L112
Franklin Library, University of Pennsylvania Libraries

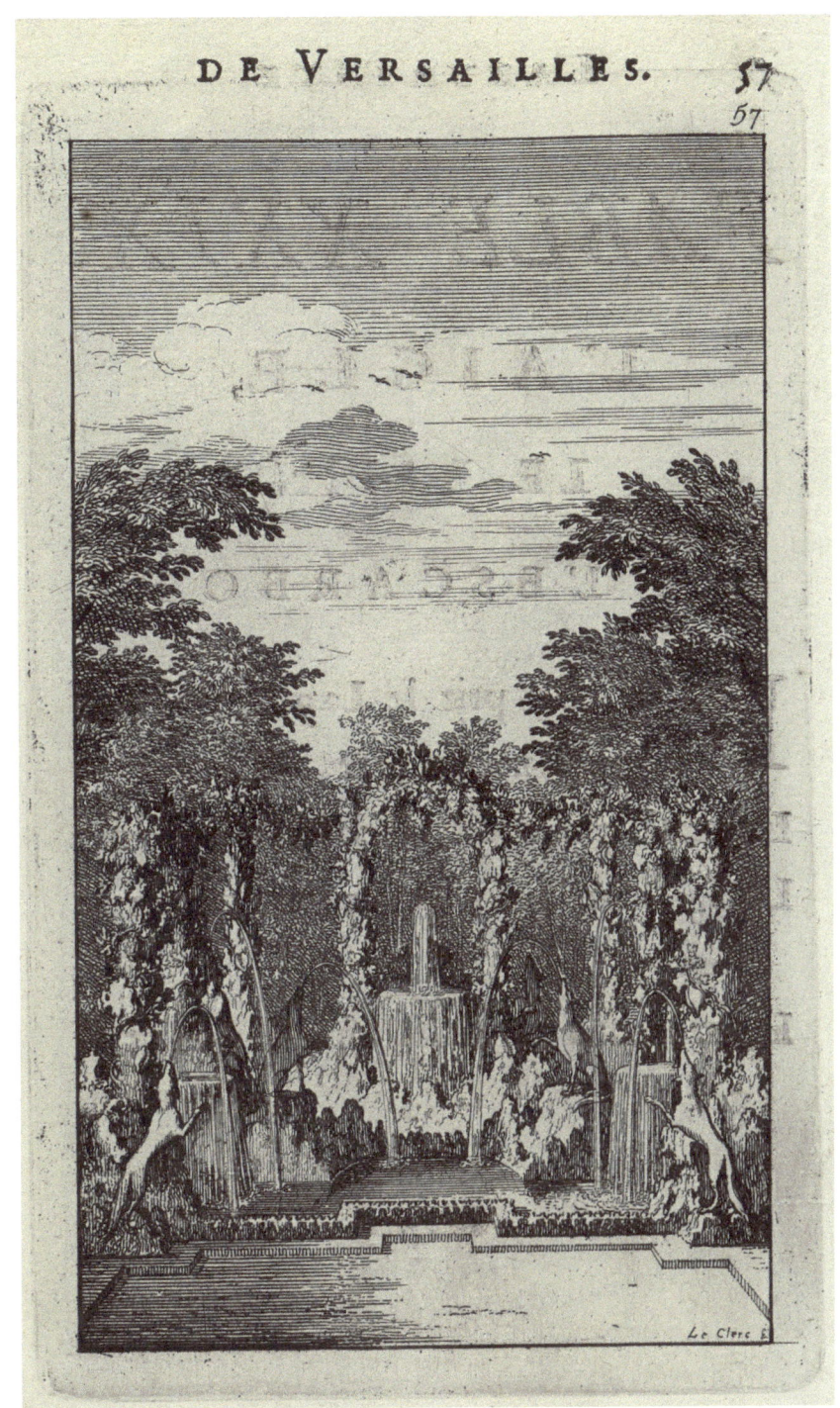

Fig. 6
Sébastien Le Clerc
Fountain of the Foxes and the Grapes, from *Le Labyrinthe de Versailles* (Paris, 1679), page 57, engraving
717 L112
Franklin Library, University of Pennsylvania Libraries

Bibliography

Ackley, Clifford S., ed. *Printmaking in the Age of Rembrandt*. Boston: Museum of Fine Arts, 1981.

Aesop. *The Complete Fables*. Translated and edited by Olivia Temple and Robert K.G. Temple. New York: Penguin Books, 1998.

Alexander, David. "'After-Images': A Review of Recent Studies of Reproductive Print-Making." Oxford *Art Journal* 6, no. 1 (1983): 11-17.

Alpers, Svetlana. *Rembrandt's Enterprise: The Studio and the Market*. Chicago, University of Chicago Press, 1988.

Andrews, Keith. *Adam Elsheimer: Paintings, Drawings, Prints*. London: Phaidon, 1977.

Baldinucci, Filippo. *Notizie dei professori del disegno da Cimabue in qua*. Originally published 1681-1728. Edited by Paola Barocchi and Antonio Boschetto. 7 Volumes. Florence: S.P.E.S., 1974.

Baldwin, Robert. "'On earth we are beggars, as Christ himself was': The Protestant Background of Rembrandt's Imagery of Poverty, Disability, and Begging." *Konsthistorisk Tidskrift* 56, no. 3 (1985): 122-135.

Baridon, Michel. *A History of the Gardens of Versailles*. Translated by Adrienne Mason. Philadelphia: University of Pennsylvania Press, 2008.

Bassani, Paola. *Claude Vignon, 1593-1670*. Paris: Arthena, 1992.

Baudi di Vesme, Alessandro, and Phyllis Dearborn Massar. *Stefano della Bella, catalogue raisonné*. New York: Collectors Edition, 1971.

Bellamy, David. *Ethic Amusements*. London: W. Faden, 1796.

Bellini, Paolo. *L'opera incise di Giovanni Benedetto Castiglione*. Milan: Ripartizione cultura e spettacolo, 1982.

Bellini, Paolo. *L'opera incise di Simone Cantarini*. Milan: Comune di Milano, Ripartizione cultura e spettacolo, 1980.

Bellini, Paolo. "Stampatori e mercanti di stampe in Italia nei secoli XVI e XVII." *I quaderni del conoscitore di stampe* 26 (1975): 19-34.

Bernard, Leon. *The Emerging City: Paris in the Age of Louis XIV*. Durham: Duke University Press, 1970.

Blankert, Albert. *Ferdinand Bol (1616-1680), Rembrandt's Pupil*. Doornspijk: Davaco, 1982.

Blunt, Anthony. "The Inventor of Soft-Ground Etching: Giovanni Benedetto Castiglione." *Burlington Magazine* 113, no. 821 (1971): 472-75.

Blunt, Anthony. "The Drawings of Giovanni Benedetto Castiglione." *Journal of the Warburg and Courtauld Institutes* 8 (1945): 161-174.

Bosse, Abraham. *Sentiments sur la distinction des diverses manières de peinture, dessin et gravure et des originaux d'avec leurs copies*. Originally published 1649. Reprint. Geneve: Minkoff, 1973.

Bosse, Abraham. *Traité des manières de graver en taille douce sur l'airin par le moyen des eaux fortes et des vernix dur et mols, ensemble la façon d'en imprimer les planches et d'en construire la presse et autre choses concernant les dits arts*. Paris: chez Bosse, 1645.

Bowles, John. *Versailles Illustrated, or Divers Views of the Several Parts of the Royal Palace of Versailles; as likewise of all the Fountains, Groves, Parterras, ye Labyrinth & other ye most Beautiful Parts of the Gardens*. London: John Bowles & Son, c. 1755.

Boyer, Jean-Claude. "Claude's Rape of Europa and the painter's early French patrons." *Burlington Magazine* 146, no. 1213 (2004): 261-63.

Brennan, Michael. *The Origins of the Grand Tour: the travels of Robert Montagu, Lord Mandeville (1649-54), William Hammond (1655-58) and Banaster Maynard (1660-63)*. London: Hayluyt Society, 2005.

Brown, Jonathan. *Jusepe de Ribera: prints and drawings*. Princeton: Princeton University, 1973.

Camille, Michael. *Gothic Art, Glorious Visions*. New York: Harry N. Abrams, 1996.

Chapman, H. Perry. *Rembrandt's Self-Portraits: A Study in Seventeenth-Century Identity*. Princeton: Princeton University Press, 1990.

Ciletti, Elena. "Judith Imagery as Catholic Orthodoxy in Counter-Reformation Italy. " In *The Sword of Judith: Judith Studies across the Disciplines*, edited by Kevin R. Brine, Elena Ciletti, and Henrike Lähnemann, 345-68. Cambridge: Open Book, 2010.

Cole, Michael, ed. *The Early Modern Painter-Etcher*. University Park: The Pennsylvania State University Press, 2006.

Cole, Michael, and Larry Silver, "Fluid Boundaries: Formations of the Painter-Etcher." In *The Early Modern Painter-Etcher*, edited by Michael Cole, 4-35. University Park: Pennsylvania State University Press, 2006.

Consagra, Francesca. "The Marketing of Pietro Testa's 'Poetic Inventions'." In *Pietro Testa, 1612-1650: Prints and Drawings*, edited by Elizabeth Cropper, lxxxvii-ci. Philadelphia: Philadelphia Museum of Art, 1988.

Crenshaw, Paul. *Bankruptcy: The Artist, His Patrons, and the Art World in Seventeenth-Century Netherlands*. Cambridge: Cambridge University Press, 2006.

Cruyl, Lieven. *Prospectus Locorum Urbis Romae insignium*. Rome: Giovanni Giacomo de' Rossi, 1666.

Daniel, Howard. *Callot's Etchings*. New York: Dover, 1974.

De Vries, Jan, and Ad van der Woude. *The First Modern Economy: Success, Failure, and Perseverance of the Dutch Economy, 1500-1815*. Cambridge: Cambridge University Press, 1997.

Dixon, Laurinda. *Perilous Chastity: Women and Illness in Pre-Enlightenment Art and Medicine*. Ithaca: Cornell University Press, 1995.

Faucheux, Louis Étienne. *Catalogue raisonné de toutes les estampes qui forment l'oeuvre d' Israël Silvestre, précédé d'une notice sur sa vie*. Paris: F. De Nobele, 1969.

Ferguson, George. *Signs and Symbols in Christian Art*. New York: Oxford University Press, 1954.

Ficacci, Luigi, ed. *Claude Mellan, gli anni romani. Un incisore tra Vouet e Bernini*. Rome: Multigrafica Editrice, 1989.

Fowle, Geraldine E. "Sébastien Bourdon's *Acts of Mercy*: Their Significance as a Series." In *Hortus Imaginum: Essays in Western Art*, edited by Robert Enggass and Marilyn Stokstad, 147-154. Lawrence: University of Kansas, 1975.

Godefroy, Louis. *The Complete Etchings of Adriaen Van Ostade*. Originally published 1930. Reprint. San Francisco: Alan Wofsy Fine Arts, 1990.

Godfrey, Richard. *Wencelaus Hollar: A Bohemian Artist in England*. New Haven and London: Yale University Press, 1994.

Goldstein, Carl. *Print Culture in Early Modern France: Abraham Bosse and the Purposes of Print*. New York: Cambridge University, 2012.

Gustot, Pierre, and Sabine van Sprang. *Gilles Neyts: un paysagiste Brabançon en Vallée Mosane au XVIIe siècle*. Namur, Belgium: Société archéologique de Namur, 2008.

Held, Julius. *Rembrandt and the Book of Tobit*. Northampton, MA: Gehenna Press, 1964.

Hind, Arthur M. *Van Dyck, his Original Etchings and his Iconography*. Boston: Houghton Mifflin, 1915.

Hind, Arthur M. *Wencelaus Hollar and his views of London and Windsor in the seventeenth century*. New York: H. Blom, 1972.

Hinterding, Erik, Ger Luijten and Martin Royalton-Kisch. *Rembrandt the Printmaker*. Chicago and London: Fitzroy Dearborn Publishers, 2000.

Hults, Linda C. *The Print in the Western World: an Introductory History*. Madison: University of Wisconsin Press, 1996.

Jatta, Barbara. *Lieven Cruyl e la sua opera graphica: un artista fiammingo nell'Italia del Seicento*. Bruxelles: Institut historique belge de Rome, 1992.

Jatta, Barbara, and Joseph Connors. *Vedute romane di Lieven Cruyl: paesaggio urbano sotto Alessandro VII*. Rome: Accademia Americana in Roma, 1989.

Join-Lambert, Sophie, and Maxime Préaud. *Abraham Bosse: savant graveur: Tours, vers 1604-1676*. Paris: Bibliothèque Nationale, 2004.

Kahn, Gerald. *Jacques Callot: Artist of the Theater*. Athens: University of Georgia Press, 1976.

Kitson, Michael. "Claude's earliest 'Coast Scene with the Rape of Europa'." *Burlington Magazine* 115, no. 849 (Dec. 1973): 775-77.

Klessman, Rüdiger, Emilie E.S. Gordenker and Christian Tico Seifert. *Adam Elsheimer 1578-1610*. Edinburgh: National Gallery of Scotland, 2006.

Knaap, Anna C. "From Lowlife to Rustic Idyll: the Peasant Genre in 17th-Century Dutch Drawings and Prints." *Harvard University Art Museums Bulletin* 4, no. 2 (spring 1996): 30-59.

Krautheimer, Richard. *The Rome of Alexander VII, 1655-1667*. Princeton: Princeton University Press, 1987.

Le Clerc, Sébastien. *Oeuvres choisies de Sébastien Le Clerc, chevalier romain, dessinateur et graveur du cabinet du roi, contenant 239 estampes, dessinées et gravées par ce célèbre artiste, représentant des costumes, des fables, des paysages, et autres objets intéressant*. Paris: chez Lamy, 1784.

Logan, Anne-Marie. *The 'Cabinet' of the Brothers Gerard and Jan Reynst*. Amsterdam: North-Holland Publishing Company, 1979.

Luijten, Ger. "The Iconography: Van Dyck's Portraits in Print." In *Anthony Van Dyck as a printmaker*, edited by Carl Depauw and Ger Luijten, 72-91. Amsterdam: Rijksmuseum, 1999.

MacQuarrie, Kim. *The Last Days of the Incans*. New York: Simon and Schuster, 2007.

Malvasia, Carlo Cesare. *Felsina pittrice: vite dei pittori bolognesi*. Originally published 1678. Edited by Marcella Brascaglia. Bologna: ALFA, 1971.

Mannocci, Lino. *The Etchings of Claude Lorrain*. New Haven and London: Yale University Press, 1989.

Markey, Lia. "The Female Printmaker and the Culture of the Reproductive Print Workshop." In *Paper Museums: The Reproductive Print in Europe 1500-1800*, edited by Rebecca Zorach and Elizabeth Rodini, 51-75. Chicago: University of Chicago, 2005.

Martin, John Rupert. *Baroque*. New York: Harper & Row, 1977.

Massar, Phyllis Dearborn. *Presenting Stefano della Bella: Seventeenth-Century Printmaker*. New York: Metropolitan Museum of Art, 1971.

Massari, Stefania. *Incisori Mantovani del '500: Giovan Battista, Adamo, Diana Scultori e Giorgio Ghisi dalle collezioni del Gabinetto Nazionale delle Stampe e della Calcografia Nazionale*. Rome: De Luca Editore, 1981.

Matthew, W.H. *Mazes and Labyrinths: their history and development*. Originally published 1922. Reprint. London: Dover, 1970.

Mauquoy-Hendrickx, Marie. *L'iconographie d'Antonie van Dyck: catalogue raisonné*. 2nd Revised Edition. 2 Volumes. Bruxelles: Bibliothèque Royale Albert I, 1991.

McTighe, Sheila. "Abraham Bosse and the Language of Artisans: Genre and Perspective in the Académie royale de peinture et de sculpture, 1648-70." *Oxford Art Journal* 21, no. 1 (1998): 1-26.

Meaume, Édouard. *Sébastien Le Clerc 1637-1714 et son oeuvre gravé: étude biographique et catalogue raisonné*. Originally published 1877. Reprint. Amsterdam: Hissink, 1969.

Minonzio, Donata and Paolo Bellini. *L'opera incisa di Giovanni Benedetto Castiglione*. Milan: Ripartizione cultura e spettacolo, 1982.

Modesti, Adelina. *Elisabetta Sirani: Una Virtuosa del Seicento Bolognese*. Bologna: Editrice Compositori, 2004.

Moffitt, John F., Sheldon Richmond and David Carrier. "On Pictures Within Pictures." *Leonardo* 12, no. 4 (Autumn, 1979): 350-51.

Montanari, Tomaso. "Bellori and Christina of Sweden." In *Art History in the Age of Bellori: Scholarship and Cultural Politics in Seventeenth-Century Rome*, edited by Janis Bell and Thomas Willette, 94-126. Cambridge: Cambridge University Press, 2002.

Muizelaar, Klaske, and Derek Phillips, *Picturing Men and Women in the Dutch Golden Age: Paintings and People in Historical Perspective.* New Haven: Yale University Press, 2003.

Mussini, Massimo. *La Bibbia di Raffaello: Scienza e scrittura nella stampa di riproduzione dei secoli XVI e XVII.* Brescia: Paideia, 1979.

Neil, Philip, and Nicoletta Simborowski. *The Complete Fairy Tales of Charles Perrault.* Boston: Houghton Mifflin Harcourt, 1993.

Orenstein, Nadine. "Marketing prints to the Dutch Republic: Novelty and the print publisher." *Journal of Medieval and Early Modern Studies* 23 (winter 1983): 141-165.

Pace, Claire. "'The Golden Age…The First and Last Days of Mankind': Claude Lorrain and the Classical Pastoral with special emphasis on themes from Ovid's Metamorphoses." *Artibus et Historiae* 23, no. 46 (2002): 127-156.

Panofsky, Erwin. *Idea: A Concept in Art Theory.* Translated by Joseph Peake. Columbia: University of South Carolina Press, 1968.

Papi, Gianni. *Orazio Borgianni.* Soncino: Edizioni dei Soncino, 1993.

Pennington, Richard. *A Descriptive Catalogue of the Etched Work of Wencelaus Hollar 1607-1677.* Cambridge, Cambridge University Press, 1982.

Percy, Anne. *Giovanni Battista Castiglione: Master Draughtsman of the Italian Baroque.* Philadelphia: Philadelphia Museum of Art, 1970.

Perlove, Shelly and Larry Silver. *Rembrandt's Faith: Church and Temple in the Dutch Golden Age.* University Park: Pennsylvania State University Press, 2009.

Perrault, Charles. *Le Labyrinthe de Versailles.* Originally published 1677. Reprint. Preface by Michel Conan. Paris: du Moniteur, 1982.

Petrucci, Alfredo. *Il Caravaggio acquafortista e il mondo calcografico romano: L'Indovina, Leoni, Borgianni, Maggi, Villamena, Onofri, Mercati, Amici di Caravaggio.* Rome: Fratelli Palombi, 1956.

Pinkney, Jerry. *Aesop's Fables.* New York: SeaStar Books, 2000.

Pon, Lisa. "Prints and Privileges: Regulating the Image in 16th-Century Italy." *Harvard University Art Museums Bulletin* 6, no. 2 (1998): 40-54.

Pon, Lisa. *Raphael, Dürer, and Marcantonio Raimondi: Copying and the Italian Renaissance Print.* New Haven: Yale University Press, 2004.

Posner, Donald. "Jacques Callot and the Dances Called Sfessania." *The Art Bulletin* 59, no. 2 (1977): 203-216.

Préaud, Maxime, and Barbara Brejon de Lavergnée. *L'Oiel d'or: Claude Mellan 1598-1688.* Paris: Bibliothèque nationale, 1988.

Reed, Sue Welsh. "Giovanni Benedetto Castiglione's 'God Creating Adam': The First Masterpiece in the Monotype Medium." *Art Institute of Chicago Museum Studies* 17, no. 1 (1991): 66-73, 94-95.

Reed, Sue Welsh, and Richard Wallace. *Italian Etchers of the Renaissance and Baroque.* Boston: Museum of Fine Arts, 1989.

Riggs, Timothy A., and Larry Silver. *Graven Images: the Rise of Professional Printmakers in Antwerp and Haarlem.* Evanston, IL: Northwestern University Press, 1993.

Robinson, William W. "'This Passion for Prints': Collecting and Connoisseurship in Northern Europe during the Seventeenth Century." In *Printmaking in the Age of Rembrandt,* edited by Clifford S. Ackley, vvvii-xlvii. Boston: Museum of Fine Arts, 1981.

Roberts, William. "Perelle's 'Veües des plus beaux endroits de Versailles': How the Engravings contribute." *Cahiers* XI (2004): 49-50.

Röthlisberg, Marcel. *Abraham Bloemaert and his sons: paintings and prints.* Doornspijk: Davaco, 1993.

Röthlisberger, Marcel. "The Perelles." *Master Drawings* 5, no. 3 (1967): 283-85, 332-33.

Rosen, Jochai. *Soldiers at Leisure: the Guardroom Scene in Dutch Genre Painting of the Golden Age.* Amsterdam: Amsterdam University Press, 2010.

Russell, Helen Diane. *Claude Lorrain, 1600-1682.* New York: George Braziller, 1982.

Russell, Helen Diane, and Jeffrey Blanchard. *Jacques Callot: Prints and Related Drawings.* Washington, DC: National Gallery of Art, 1975.

Schama, Simon. *Rembrandt's Eyes*. New York: Alfred A. Knopf, 1999.

Schiller, Gertrud. *Iconography of Christian Art*. 2 Volumes. New York: New York Graphic Society, 1971.

Schuckman, Christiaan, Martin Royalton-Kisch, and Erick Hinterding. *Rembrandt and Van Vliet: A Collaboration on Copper*. Amsterdam: Rembrandhuis, 1996.

Schwartz, Gary. *Rembrandt's Universe: his life, his art, his world*. London: Thames and Hudson, 2006.

Scott, Dorothea. *Perrault and Aesop's Fables*. Baltimore: Johns Hopkins University Press, 1982.

Scott, Jonathan. *Salvator Rosa: His Life and Times*. New Haven and London: Yale University Press, 1995.

Simone, Kate. *Renaissance Tapestry: the Gonzaga of Mantua*. New York: Harper and Row, 1988.

Sonnabend, Martin. "Claude Lorrain: the Printmaker." In *Claude Lorrain: The Enchanted Landscape*, edited by Martin Sonnabend and John Whiteley, 137-149. Oxford: Ashmolean Museum, 2011.

Sonnabend, Martin and John Whiteley, eds. *Claude Lorrain: the Enchanted Landscape*. Oxford: Ashmolean Museum, 2011.

Sopher, Marcus S., and Claudia Lazzaro. *Seventeenth-Century Prints*. Stanford: Stanford Art Gallery, 1978.

Standring, Timothy J., and Martin Clayton. *Castiglione: Lost Genius*. London: Royal Collection Trust, 2013.

Stone-Ferrier, Linda. *Dutch Prints of Daily Life: Mirrors of Life or Masks of Morals?* Lawrence, KS: University of Kansas Press, 1983.

Thompson, Ian. *The Sun King's Garden: Louis XIV, Andre Le Notre and the Creation of the Gardens of Versailles*. New York: Bloomsbury, 2006.

Thornton, Peter. *Seventeenth-Century Interior Decoration in England, France and Holland*. New Haven: Yale University Press, 1979.

Thuillier, Jacques. *Sébastien Bourdon, 1616-1671: catalogue critique et chronologique de l'oeuvre complet*. Paris: Réunion des musées nationaux, 2000.

van den Boogaart, Ernst. "De Brys' Africa." In *Inszenierte Welten: Die west und ostindischen Reisen der Verleger de Bry, 1590-1630*, edited by Susanna Burghartz, 95-155. Basel: Schwabe, 2004.

van der Coelen, Peter, Theo Laurentius, S. William Pelletier, Tom Rassieur, and Leonard J. Slatkes. *Everyday Life in Holland's Golden Age: The Complete Etchings of Adriaen van Ostade*. Amsterdam: Museum het Rembrandthuis, 1998.

Van Eerde, Katherine S. *Wencelaus Hollar: Delineator of his Times*. Charlottesville: University Press of Virginia, 1970.

van Linschoten, Jan Huygen. *Itinerario: Voyage ofte schipvaert van Jan Huyghen van Linschoten naer Oost ofte Portugaels Indien*. Amsterdam: Cornelis Claesz, 1596.

Wallace, Richard. *The Etchings of Salvator Rosa*. Princeton: Princeton University Press, 1979.

Walton, Guy. *Louis XIV's Versailles*. Chicago: University Chicago Press, 1986.

Weiss, Allen. *Mirrors of Infinity: the French Formal Garden and 17th-Century Metaphysics*. New York: Princeton Architectural Press, 1995.

Westermann, Mariët. *A Worldly Art: The Dutch Republic, 1585-1718*. New York: Harry N. Abrams, 1996.

Westermann, Mariët, C. Willemijn Fock, Eric van Sluijer and H. Perry Chapman. *Art and Home: Dutch Interiors in the Age of Rembrandt*. Zwolle: Waanders, 2000.

Wheelock, Arthur, Susan Barnes and Julius Held. *Anthony Van Dyck, 1599-1641*. Washington, DC: National Gallery of Art, c. 1990.

White, Christopher. *Anthony Van Dyck: Thomas Howard, The Earl of Arundel*. Malibu, CA: Getty Publications, 1995.

White, Christopher, and Karel G. Boon. *Rembrandt's Etchings: an illustrated critical catalogue*. 2 Volumes. Amsterdam: Van Gendt & Co, 1969.

Wölfflin, Heinrich. *Principles of Art History: The Problem of the Development of Style in Later Art.* Originally Published 1915. Translated by M. D. Hottinger. New York: Dover Publications, 1932.

Zorbach, Rebecca. "'A secret kind of charm not to be explained or discerned': On Claude Mellan's Insinuating Line." *RES: Anthropology and Aesthetics 55/66: Absconding* (spring/autumn 2009): 235-51.

Zorach, Rebecca, and Elizabeth Rodini, eds. *Paper Museums: The Reproductive Print in Europe 1500-1800.* Chicago: University of Chicago, 2005.

Appendix A:

Catalogue of Artworks

Printmakers of the Baroque:
17th-Century Explorations of Space and Light

La Salle University Art Museum

Labels researched and written by Olivia Abney (OA), Chikenye (Kiki) Akpunonu (KA), Daniel Biester (DB), Rachel Christie (RC), Taylor Colaiacovo (TC), Marlana Dalessandro (MD), Susan Dixon (SD), Sarah Finn (SF), Elisabeth Giraud (EG), Amanda Hershock (AH), Amanda Martinez (AM), Irene Martinez (IM), Holly Michaels (HM), Megan Rankel (MR), Kelly Sheehan (KS), Taylor Strickland (TS), Emily Tomlin (ET), and Alonda White (AW).

Introduction to the Exhibition

By the 1970s, the long-held Wölfflinian principles of defining Baroque art were reconsidered and found wanting. Heinrich Wölfflin, writing in 1915, had employed formal qualities as means to determine the distinctiveness of Baroque art, known for its drama and mystery. Defining his terms, he argued that it was painterly rather than linear in its presentation; it was open rather than closed in form, etc.[1] Although these were useful categories, they had severe limitations. In 1977, John Rupert Martin provided an alternative means of understanding the art of 17th-century Europe. In a well-known book simply entitled *Baroque*, he proposed that "we must look for… the embodiment of certain widely held ideas, attitudes and assumptions".[2] He laid out larger themes that were explored and expressed well in most Baroque works of art. The two most striking are space and light.[3] Martin believed that the unification of space, in which "everything forms part of a continuous and unbroken reality," was a scientific tenet, a religious belief, and an artistic aim of the period.[4] It was achieved equally in the works of Gianlorenzo Bernini and Johannes Vermeer. Observations of light and its counterpart shadow were also symptoms of the 17th-century impulse to see the world wholistically. Baroque artists as diverse as Caravaggio and Nicholas Poussin responded to that impulse. The goal of the exhibition is to illustrate and elaborate on these themes as they are found in the print culture of the Baroque. SD

1   Heinrich Wolfflin, *Principles of Art History: The Problem of the Development of Style in Later Art (1915)*, trans. M. D. Hottinger (New York: Dover Publications, 1932). There have been various reprints. The last 3 categories were recessive versus linear; multiplicity versus unity; and absolute versus relative clarity.

2   John Rupert Martin, *Baroque* (New York: Harper & Row), 1977, 12. Other themes include Time, Naturalism, Passions of the Soul, Attitudes towards Antiquity, and Transcendental Views of Reality.

3   Ibid., 155-196; and 223-48, respectively.

4   Ibid., 155.

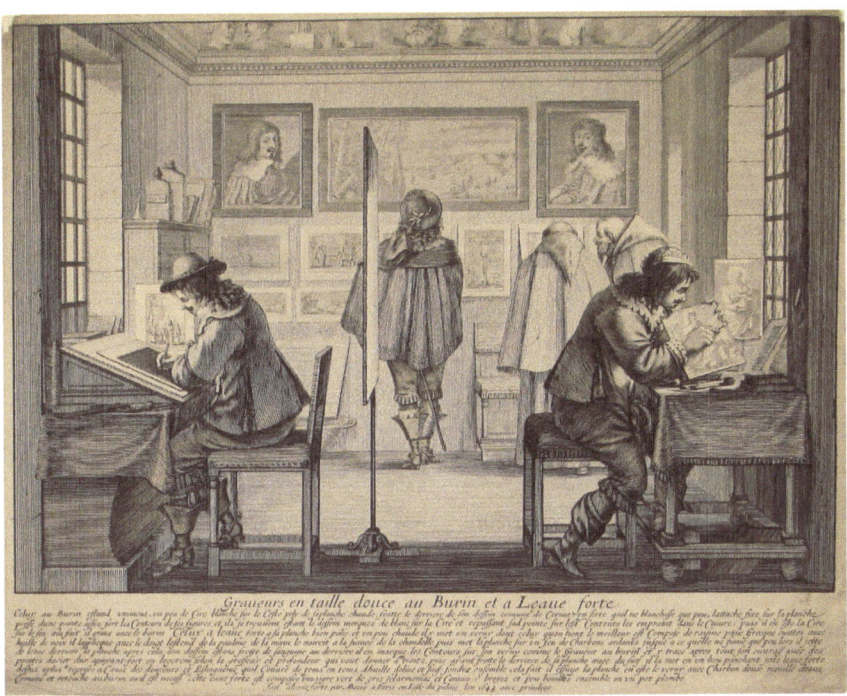

Cat. 1
Abraham Bosse (1602-1676), French
The Etcher and Engraver, 1643
10 1/8" x 12 1/2"
Etching
81-G-1119

Bosse depicts a 17th-century French print shop in great detail. To the right is the engraver, working his metal plate with a burin. He reproduces an image of the Madonna and Child. To the right is the etcher, whose plate is covered with an acid-resistant ground, into which he draws the design with an etching needle. Prints are on display against the wall for discerning clients: the nobleman and the two monks. The printed images are diverse and include religious subjects, landscapes, and political broadsheets.[1]

Bosse was an advocate for the elevated status of the print-making profession in France. His 1645 treatise on the methods of engraving and etching, *Traité des manières de graver en taille douce*, was the first of its kind.[2] It promoted good technique and work habits among all those involved in printmaking.

For his efforts, the printmaker was accepted into the Académie royale, the academy of the fine arts of painting and sculpture, in 1648, to teach perspective. Bosse's arguments for the dignity of the profession, however, were complex. He did not call for elevating the status of print-making to a liberal art, or an activity of the mind, an argument that ennobled the arts of painting and sculpture. Rather, he underscored the idea that printmaking was an essential manual labor that required integrity.[3] His extensive and diverse *oeuvre*, which includes many prints of a practical nature (e.g., book illustrations, fashion plates and military scenes) attests to his commitment to that idea.[4] The feisty Bosse's polemics did not always sit easily with his fellow academicians. He was formally ousted from the Academy in 1661.[5] IM, SF

1   Carl Goldstein, *Print Culture in Early Modern France: Abraham Bosse and the Purposes of Print* (New York: Cambridge University, 2012), 15-18.

2   *Traité des manières de graver en taille douce sur l'airin par le moyen des eaux fortes et des vernix dur et mols, ensemble la façon d'en imprimer les planches et d'en construire la presse et autre choses concernant les dits arts* (Paris: chez Bosse, 1645). It explained the new methods of etching as practiced by Jacques Callot (see cat. 11 in this catalogue).

3   Goldstein, *Print Culture in Early Modern France*, 22-24.

4   Sophie Join-Lambert and Maxime Préaud, *Abraham Bosse: savant graveur: Tours, vers 1604-1676* (Paris: Bibliothèque Nationale, 2004).

5   Sheila McTighe, "Abraham Bosse and the Language of Artisans: Genre and Perspective in the Académie royale de peinture et de sculpture, 1648-70," *Oxford Art Journal* 21, no. 1 (1998): 1-26.

Space

Exuberant spatial illusions are a hallmark of much 17th-century European art. Exploiting the rules of linear perspective, invented in the 1400s to create convincing spatial illusions on a flat surface, some artists created the appearance of accelerated views into deeply engrossing spaces. The famous ceiling frescoes exemplify this type of Baroque art. The viewer is impressed, even overwhelmed, by the limitlessness of his/her surroundings. Artists also manipulated the viewpoint, the imagined point at which the viewer must stand to take in the depicted world. By placing the viewpoint too high, too low, too close, or off to one side, they played with the viewers' response to what is depicted. All this creates the emotional appeal of Baroque art.

Depictions of real and imagined spaces proliferate in the Baroque period. Completing a trend begun in the 16th century, landscape became an art subject in its own right. Initially, artists used it as grandiose backdrops for the actions of mortals and immortals. Later the landscape itself, with its distinctive trees, hillocks or clouds, came to embody the human psyche. Furthermore, increased travel during this century made Europeans aware of places in and beyond their continent. Views of Rome's magnificent churches, Versailles' extraordinary gardens, and the cityscapes of London and Prague become art subjects. They functioned as alluring evocations for those who had traveled and curiosities for those who had not.

17th-century Europeans experienced the expansion of their world. Explorers and merchants, particularly from Spain and Portugal, set out for the Americas, Africa and beyond. The Dutch East India Company set up lasting colonies in parts of Africa by the mid-17th century, and traded expansively in Asia. In addition, after the Protestant Reformation in northern Europe, Catholic missionaries led by the Jesuits dispersed to India and China.

They all served as conduits for knowledge and material goods from these exotic places back to Europe. European perceptions of the indigenous people they encountered are recorded in various books and prints. Such images were beguiling and thus popular, but they often convey gross stereotypes and prejudices.

In addition, those who lived at the margins of society received the keen attention of certain Baroque artists. Depictions of peasants, or people from the countryside, which had first been seen in the 16th century, became more numerous. Soldiers, too, appear more frequently in art than in earlier centuries. The off-duty soldier is illustrated as existing, sometimes awkwardly, in society's civilized spaces: the church, the square, the inn, and the household. Furthermore, "tronies", or character heads of people with unusual features and exotic costumes, were fashionable at this time, both in Northern and Southern Europe. They express a probing fascination with those from different parts of the world. SD

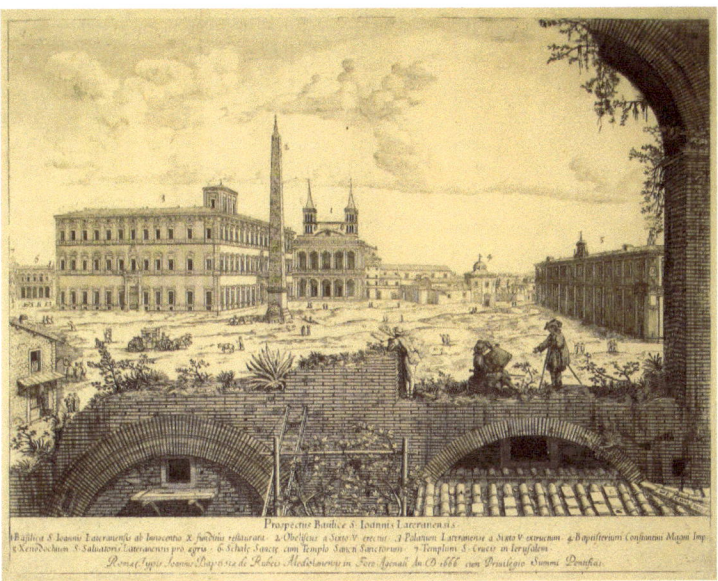

Cat. 2
Lieven Cruyl (c. 1640-c. 1720), Flemish
View of St. John Lateran, Rome, c. 1664-66
From *Prospectus Locorum Urbis Romae insignium* (Rome:
Giovanni Giacomo de' Rossi, 1666)
14 3/4" x 18 3/4"
Etching and engraving
76-G-613

The Lateran Palace and its adjacent church, Saint John Lateran, is the seat of the Bishop of Rome, who is the Pope. It is the site second in importance to the Vatican Palace and St. Peter's Cathedral. This print depicts the palace with its benediction loggia (the balcony from which blessings are given to the crowd) in the background. The Egyptian obelisk in the large square in front of the loggia was brought by the ancient Romans from Alexandria in 10 B.C. and erected at the Lateran Palace in 1606.

Cruyl, a Flemish prelate, visited Rome from around 1664 to 1672 to study optical sciences.[1] This was during a major rebuilding of the city under Pope Alexander VII Chigi (reigned 1655-1667).[2] While there, Cruyl practiced his skills at perspective, and he drew and cut 23 plates of the city's most remarkable sites which were bound and published together.[3] He created no other etchings after he left Rome.

Cruyl is known for his accuracy in capturing the site, both in building placement and in architectural detail.[4] The front façade of the church of St. John Lateran is not depicted because it sits at a 90 degree angle from the palace. However, we do see two smaller structures. The façade of the Scala Sancta, said to be the stair Christ ascended when he was brought before Pontius Pilate, is in the far left distance, while the small octagonal building, the Baptistry, believed to be where the Emperor Constantine was baptized, is to the right of the loggia.

The design in the foreground alludes to the decay of the city that precipitated its major reconstruction in the Baroque period. One of the figures is shown sketching the view atop the repurposed ruins of one of the ancient aqueducts.[5] SD

1   Barbara Jatta, *Lieven Cruyl e la sua opera graphica: un artista fiammingo nell'Italia del Seicento* (Bruxelles: Institut historique belge de Rome, 1992), 10.

2   Barbara Jatta and Joseph Connors, *Vedute romane di Lieven Cruyl: paesaggio urbano sotto Alessandro VII* (Rome: Accademia Americana in Roma, 1989); and Richard Krautheimer, *The Rome of Alexander VII, 1655-1667* (Princeton: Princeton University Press, 1987). Pope Alexander VII, however, was not interested in continuing the renovation of St. John Lateran, which had begun under the former papacy of Innocent X. See Ibid., 45.

3   Jatta, *Lieven Cruyl e la sua opera graphica*, 8-9 and 222.

4   Ibid., 15-26.

5   In a second edition of the *Prospectus Locorum Urbis Romae*, this foreground vignette was redesigned and the ruins were removed. See Ibid., 223.

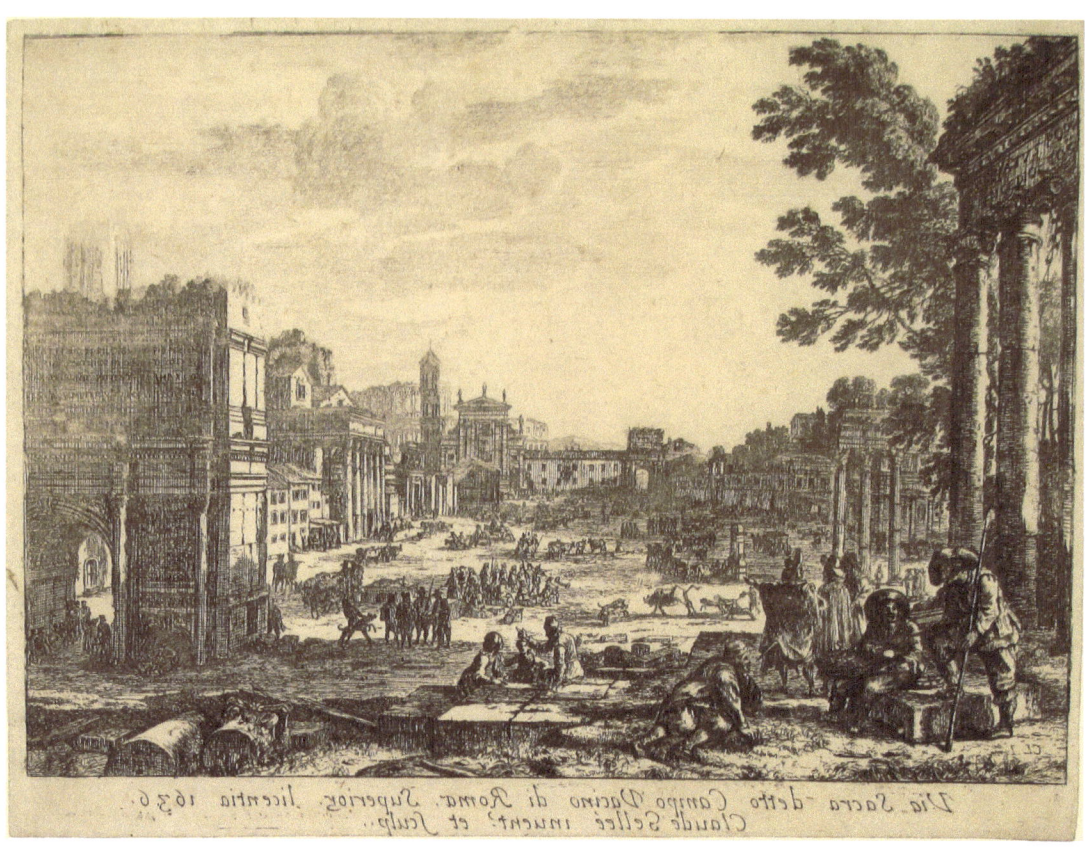

Cat. 3
Claude Lorrain (1604-1682), French
The Roman Forum, 1636
7 7/8" x 10 3/8"
Etching
07-G-3410

Claude Lorrain, commonly referred to as Claude, had a successful career in Rome creating pastoral landscape paintings. Claude's paintings and etchings are admired for capturing the luminous quality of sunlight. In his etchings, he strove to achieve the desired lighting affect by handling the etching needle in a manner that was both loose and energetic, and at the same time, tightly controlled. He took more time than most artists to make an individual etching, and he produced a total of about 40 over the course of his career, working on them on and off for over 30 years.[1]

This print reproduces Claude's own painting of the Campo Vaccino, or cow pasture, located in the ancient Roman Forum.[2] In the artist's day, the Forum had not yet been excavated.[3] Among the cows, cowherders and other more distinguished visitors to the site are the sub-

merged Arch of Septimius Severus to the right and the Arch of Titus in the far background. The image, however, reverses the placement of the structures. It is a counterproof, which is a print created when the inked paper of a recently pulled print is pressed upon another paper. Counterproofs are useful to a printmaker in helping him see where any changes to the plate should be made. AW, SD

1   Martin Sonnabend, "Claude Lorrain: the Printmaker," in Martin Sonnabend and John Whiteley, eds., *Claude Lorrain: the Enchanted Landscape* (Oxford: Ashmolean Museum, 2011), 139-141, 179-180.

2   Helen Diane Russell, *Claude Lorrain, 1600-1682* (New York: George Braziller, 1982), 349-52. His painting is now in the Louvre, Paris. The two works were dependent on Herman van Swanevelt's painting. See also Lino Mannocci, *The Etchings of Claude Lorrain* (New Haven and London: Yale University Press, 1989), 7-10, 127-137.

3   Excavations of the Roman Forum began in earnest only in the early 19th century, during the French occupation of the city.

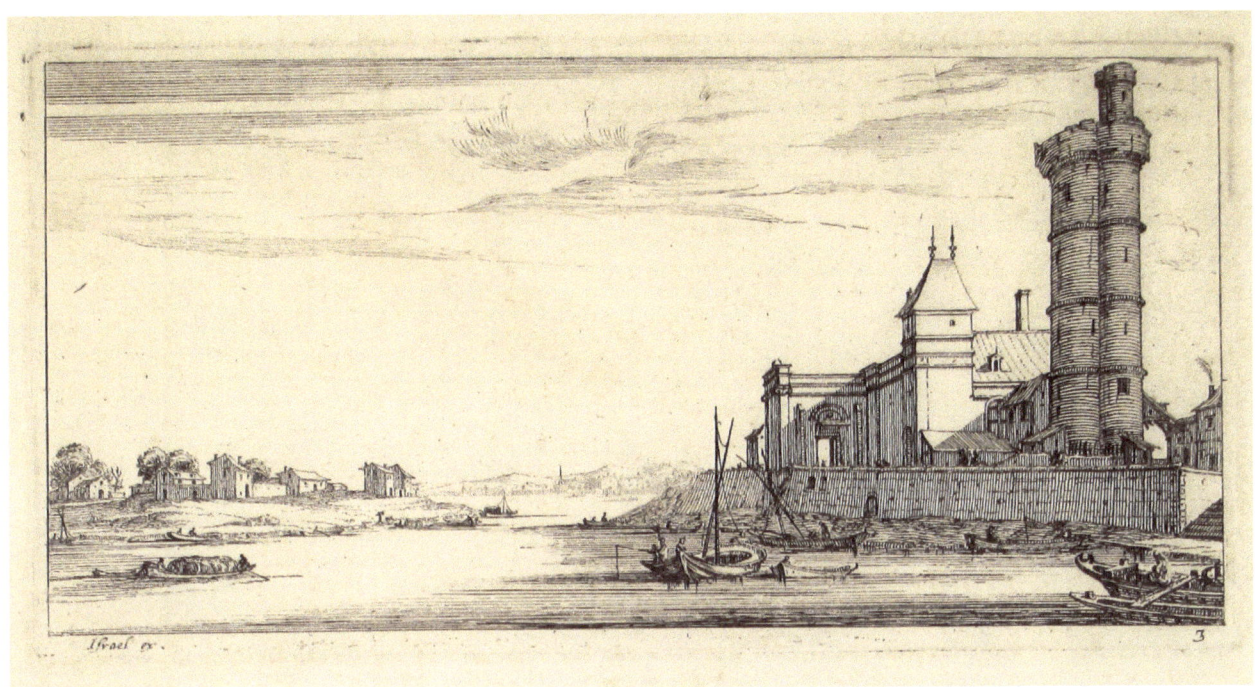

Cat. 4
Israël Silvestre (1621-1691), French
Port de Conférence
From *Vues de Paris* (Paris, c. 1660s)
2 ¹/₂" x 5 ⁷/₁₆"
Etching
77-G-767

Silvestre made over 1,000 prints, many of them views of European cities, and including Paris, the city in which he learned printmaking.[1] In this print, he captured a view of the Port de la Conférence on the right bank of the Seine River. It was located near the Tuileries Gardens, at the westernmost edge of the city, along the defensive walls. Silvestre captures the gatehouse as well as the river and those who work on it.

Today one could not find this view. After this print was made, the city was expanded under the French King Louis XIV and his Minister Colbert, and the gate and the villages beyond were obliterated. This site is now part of the Place de la Concorde, and the Champs-Élysées are west of it.[2] SD

1   On his life, see Michael Brennan, *The Origins of the Grand Tour: the travels of Robert Montagu, Lord Mandeville (1649-54), William Hammond (1655-58) and Banaster Maynard (1660-63)* (London: Hayluyt Society, 2005), 47-53. On his work, see Louis Étienne Faucheux, *Catalogue raisonné de toutes les estampes qui forment l'oeuvre d'Israël Silvestre, précédé d'une notice sur sa vie* (Paris, F. De Nobele, 1969).

2   For a sense of the changing city, see Leon Bernard, *The Emerging City: Paris in the age of Louis XIV* (Durham: Duke University Press, 1970), 3-28.

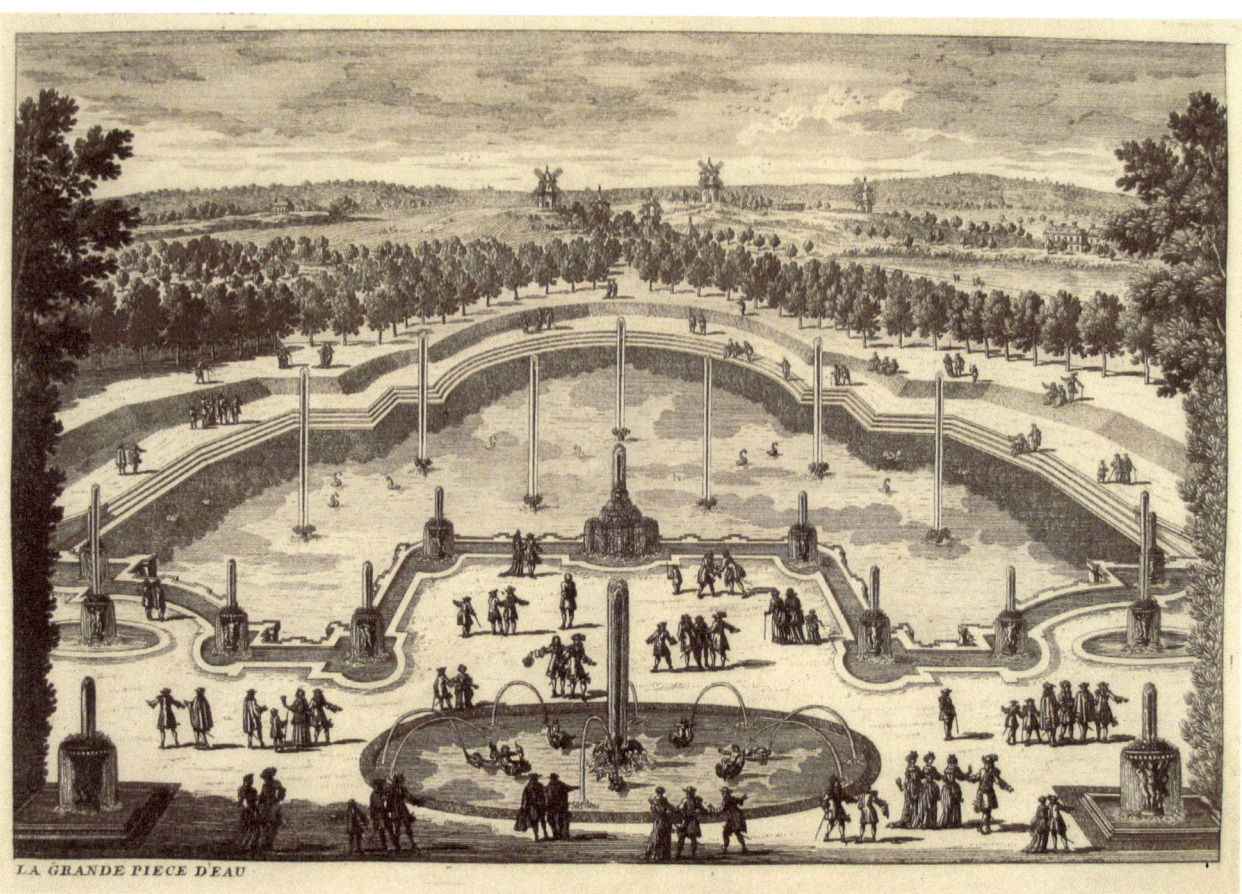

LA GRANDE PIECE D'EAU

Cat. 5
Gabriel (1603-1677), Nicolas (1631-1695), and Adam (1638-1695) Perelle, French
The Grand Water Basin
From *Vues, châteaux et maisons de France* (Paris, late 17th century)
7 7/8" x 10 3/8"
Etching and engraving
13-G-3551
Gift of Susan M. Dixon

This intricately shaped water basin is located on the east/west axis of the garden at Versailles, near King Louis XIV's palace. Created in 1676 during one of many building campaigns, it is the largest basin in the garden. Its spouts were said to shoot water 60 feet into the air, an amazing feat in that day. A statue of Neptune, which gives the basin its current name, the Neptune Basin, was added in 1740.[1]

The Perelles – father Gabriel and sons Nicolas and Adam -- were known for visually documenting the king's garden, among many sites in and around Paris.[2] Here they chose a high vantage point that creates the illusion that the site is never-ending. The endless vista is characteristic of the Baroque period, and here signals Louis XIV's aspirations for limitless power.[3] The windmill in the far background refers to the water pumps needed to keep the fountains in operation. Supplying water to the vast garden was a challenge for the hydraulic engineers at the French court.[4] HM

1   Ian Thompson, *The Sun King's Garden: Louis XIV, Andre Le Notre and the Creation of the Gardens of Versailles* (New York: Bloomsbury, 2006), 243-45.

2   Since there is little information on the artists, most scholars focus on the content of their prints. See William Roberts, "Perelle's 'Veües des plus beaux endroits de Versailles': How the Engravings contribute" *Cahiers* XI (2004): 49-50. It is difficult to distinguish among the three hands of the artists, although some scholars believe the father Gabiel's style is delicate, and Adam's style is robust and dense. See Marcel Röthlisberger, "The Perelles," *Master Drawings* 5, no. 3 (1967), 284.

3   Allen Weiss, *Mirrors of Infinity: the French Formal Garden and 17th-Century Metaphysics* (New York: Princeton Architectural Press, 1995), 61-77.

4   Thompson, *The Sun King's Garden*, 229-59.

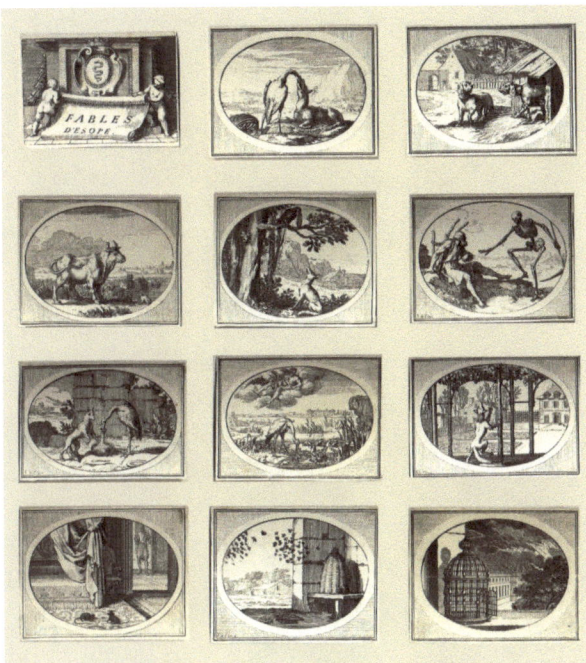

Cat. 6
Sébastien Le Clerc (1637-1714), French
Aesop's Fables
Illustrations from *Fables d'Esope* (Paris, 1683)
2 3/16" x 1 3/4" each
Engraving
85-G-1341 (Selections from 1-23)

Aesop's fables, written by a 6th-century B.C.E. Greek slave, became popular in Europe by the 15th century, and they were translated into many languages. These short stories featured talking animals and conveyed simple moral lessons. The printmaker Le Clerc created 22 illustrations for the fables, which he bound and published in 1683.[1]

Charles Perrault (1628-1703), the author of many fairy tales including *Little Red Riding Hood* and *Puss in Boots*, suggested a design for a section of King Louis XIV's garden at Versailles based on Aesop's Fables. Thus, the Labyrinth was created between 1672 and 1677.[2] It was a maze whose intersecting pathways were adorned with 39 delightful fountains, each displaying characters from one of the fables.[3] This section of the garden does not exist today. The vignettes in the small oval prints resemble the fountain designs in subject and composition. MR

First Row:

(1) Title Page, with dedication to Minister Jean-Baptiste Colbert
(17) The Wolf and the Crane
(18) The Female Dog with her puppies and the Male Dog

Second Row:

(11) The Ox and the Frog
(19) The Fox and the Crow
(23) Death and the Poor Man

Third Row:

(2) The Stork and the Fox
(13) The Frogs demanding a king from Jupiter
(16) The Fox and the Grapes

Fourth Row:

(22) The Country Mouse and the Town Mouse
(12) The Honeybee and the Hive
(7) The Bird Cage and the Escaped Bird

1   *Oeuvres choisies de Sébastien Le Clerc, chevalier romain, dessinateur et graveur du cabinet du roi, contenant 239 estampes, dessinées et gravées par ce célèbre artiste, représentant des costumes, des fables, des paysages, et autres objets intéressant* (Paris: chez Lamy), 1784, 24; and Edouard Meaume, *Sébastien Le Clerc 1637-1714 et son oeuvre gravé: étude biographique et catalogue raisonné*, originally published 1877, reprint (Amsterdam: Hissink, 1969), 140-143.

2   Charles Perrault, *Le Labyrinthe de Versailles*, originally published 1677, reprint, preface by Michel Conan (Paris: du Moniteur, 1982).

3   Ian Thompson, *The Sun King's Garden: Louis XIV, Andre Le Notre and the Creation of the Gardens of Versailles* (New York: Bloomsbury, 2006), 137-141; and Michel Baridon, *A History of the Gardens of Versailles*, trans. Adrienne Mason (Philadelphia: University of Pennsylvania Press, 2008), 184-190. For more on these fountains, see essay by Megan Rankel in this catalogue.

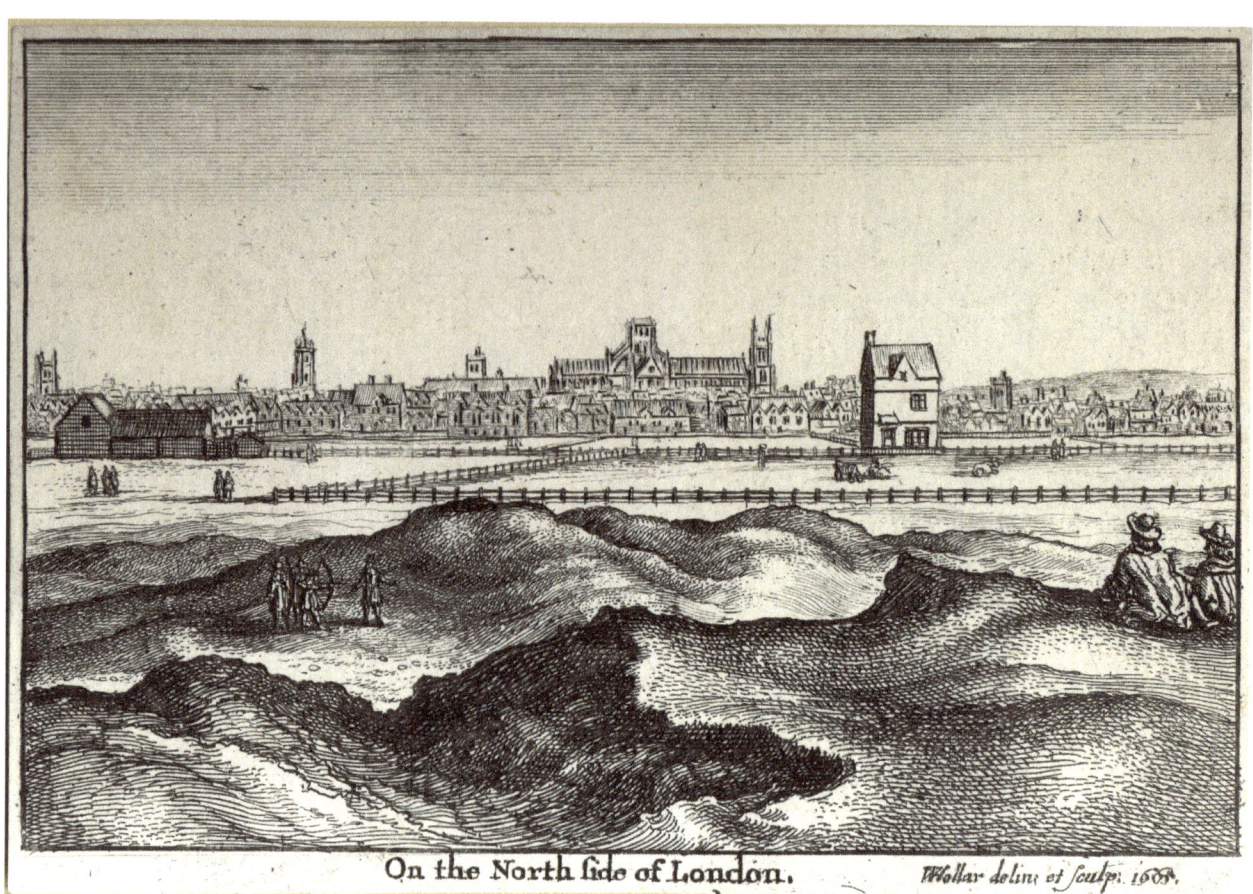

On the North fide of London.   *Wollar delin: et fculp: 1665.*

Cat. 7
Wenceslaus Hollar (1607-1677), Bohemian
On the North Side of London, 1665
3 7/8" x 2 1/2"
Etching
77-G-758

Hollar was born in Prague and because of religious persecution, he became an itinerant artist. In exile, he spent
considerable time in London. There he worked for high-
society patrons who appreciated his topographical views
with their solid architectonic forms.[1] This print captures
the bustling city, with St. Paul Cathedral at its center.
The cathedral depicted here was destroyed just a year
after the print's issue, during the Great Fire of London
in 1666. It was subsequently rebuilt to different effect on
the design of Christopher Wren. The print also describes

the countryside north of London. In an age when defensive city walls had become obsolete, the rural spaces outside the city were reconceptualized. They served not as
a home for the peasant farmer but as a temporary refuge
from the overcrowded city for the urban elite.[2] SD

1   Katherine S. Van Eerde, *Wencelaus Hollar: Delineator of his Times* (Charlottesville:
     University Press of Virginia, 1970), 44-68; and Richard Godfrey, *Wencelaus Hollar: A
     Bohemian Artist* in England (New Haven and London: Yale University Press, 1994),
     1-28. This print dates from Hollar's second stay in England.

2   Arthur M. Hind, *Wencelaus Hollar and his views of London and Windsor in the seven-
     teenth century* (New York: H. Blom, 1972), 67-68.

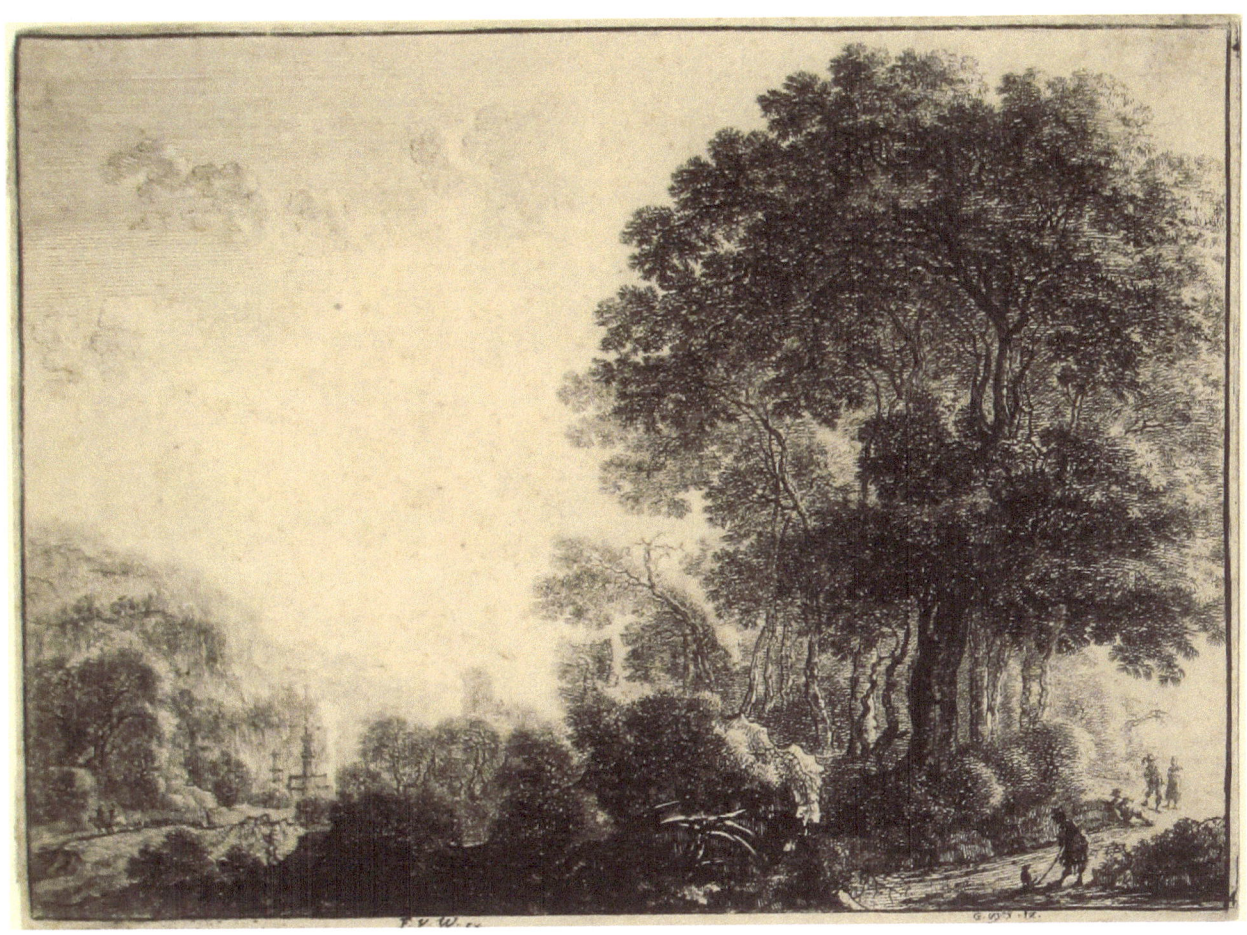

Cat. 8
Gillis Neyts (1623-1687), Flemish
Published by Frans van den Wyngaerde (1614-1679), Flemish
Man and His Dog, 17th century
5 3/16" x 6 1/4"
Etching
13-G-3584
Gift of James T. Tanis and Dr. Justin Tanis

The tangle of brush by the fallen tree at the center foreground divides the image into two, thus underscoring the different uses of the land. The eye can be led down the road to the right, dotted with well-dressed men leisurely resting or strolling under the tree. Among this group is a man walking his pet dog on a leash. Alternatively, the eye can be led to the left, where herdsmen and their flocks and herd dog can be seen outside the distant city.

Neyts is known as a prolific and talented painter and draftsman of Flemish landscape scenes, creating both imaginary scenes and specific scenes from the Mosan region.[1] However, he only created 30 prints over the course of his career. Van Den Wyngaerd was a successful printmaker and publisher who reproduced and issued the work of many of Neyts' Flemish contemporaries, including Peter Paul Rubens and Anthony van Dyck.[2] SD

1   Pierre Gustot and Sabine van Sprang, *Gilles Neyts: un paysagiste Brabançon en Vallée Mosane au XVIIe siècle* (Namur, Belgium: Société archéologique de Namur, 2008), 27-34.

2   Ibid., 262, 267. Van Den Wyngaerd published the third state of this print. The first state does not reveal any publisher's name; the second gives Joan Huysens as the publisher.

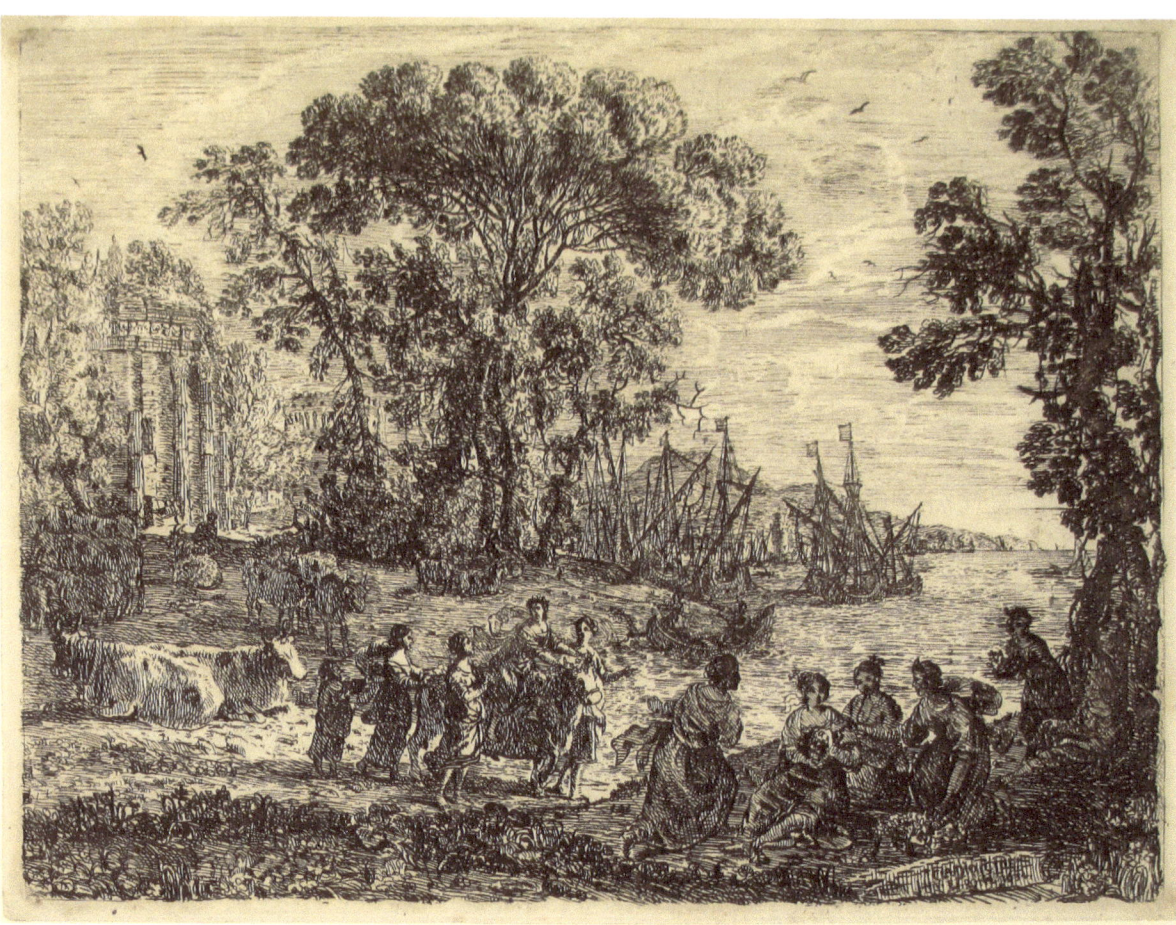

Cat. 9
Claude Lorrain (1604-1682), French
Coast Scene with Rape of Europa, 1634
7 7/8 x 10 3/8"
Etching
13-G-3585
Gift of James T. Tanis and Dr. Justin Tanis

Claude returned to the subject of the Rape of Europa many times in paintings and in prints.[1] In this early version, derived from the ancient Roman poet Ovid's *Metamorphoses*, the wealthy and beautiful maiden Europa sits calmly on the back of the god Jupiter who has taken the guise of a white bull. The dramatic part of the story, when the bull runs into the sea, abducting her and setting her on a life of exile, is not hinted at. Instead, her joyous companions gather flowers, while cows and cowherds dot the pastoral scene.

Claude's depiction of the non-dramatic moment sits within a shimmering pastoral setting. It features an an-

cient temple and mast ships moored at the coastline. The space seems more appropriate for lovers on their way to the goddess Venus' mythical island of Cythera, as in Watteau's 18th-century Rococo composition, than for the scene of a violent rape.[2] DB, SD

1   Michael Kitson, "Claude's earliest 'Coast Scene with the Rape of Europa'," *Burlington Magazine* 115, no. 849 (Dec. 1973): 775-77; and Lino Mannocchi, *The Etchings of Claude Lorrain* (New Haven and London: Yale University Press, 1989), 104-111. Jean-Claude Boyer, "Claude's Rape of Europa and the painter's early French patrons," *Burlington Magazine* 146, no. 1213 (2004): 261-63, notes that it is a reproduction of a painting of the subject now in the Kimbell Art Museum in Fort Worth, although it is different in significant ways, for example, as in the scale of the figures in the landscape. See Martin Sonnabend, "Claude Lorrain: the Printmaker," in Martin Sonnabend and John Whitely, eds., *Claude Lorrain: the Enchanted Landscape* (Oxford: Ashmolean Museum, 2011), 139-140, 170-171.

2   Claire Pace, "'The Golden Age…The First and Last Days of Mankind': Claude Lorrain and the Classical Pastoral with special emphasis on themes from Ovid's Metamorphoses," *Artibus et Historiae* 23, no. 46 (2002): 135, 146-148.

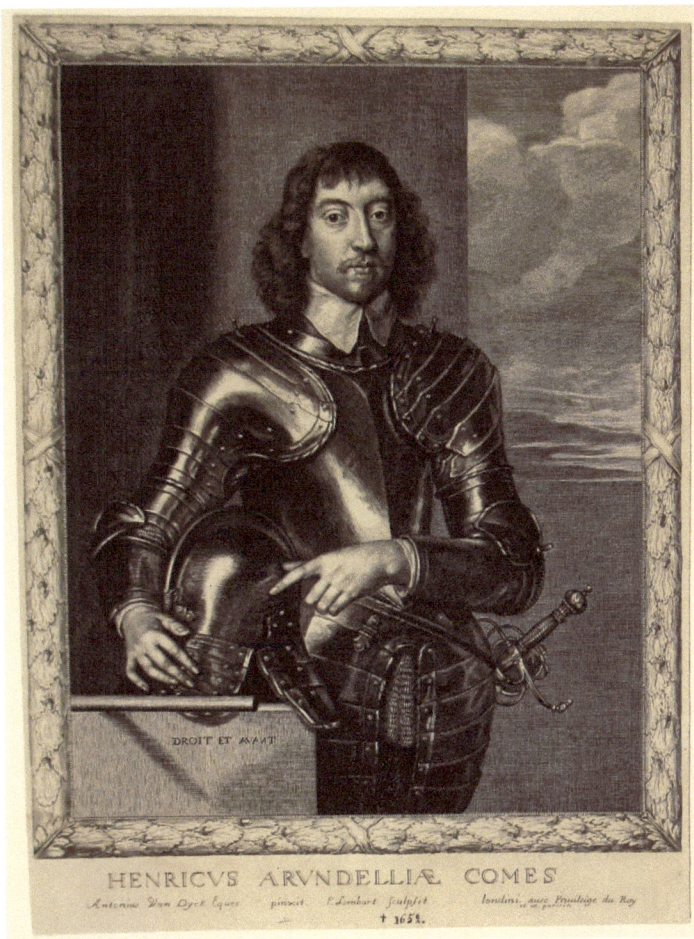

HENRICVS ARVNDELLIÆ COMES

Cat. 10
Pierre Lombart (1613-1682), French
After a drawing by Anthony Van Dyck (1599-1641), Flemish
Henry Frederick Howard, the 22nd Earl of Arundel
From an edition of *Iconographia*, 1652
13 ⅝" x 10 ⅜" (sheet)
Engraving
14-G-3658

Van Dyck had a successful career in England as well as in his native Flanders, and he was known for his stunning life-size portrait paintings.

He produced many portraits of the Arundel family, whose figurehead, Sir Thomas Howard, was one of the artist's great patrons.[1] This print after a drawing by Van Dyck is a three-quarter length portrait of Henry Frederick Howard, the 22nd Earl of Arundel, the son of Sir Thomas. He wears armor reminiscent of his father's, as captured in a portrait by Van Dyck's mentor Peter Paul Rubens.[2] His helmet sits on a column to his right. It bears an inscription that reads "Droit et Avant"("Right and Front"), surely a reference to his readiness for battle. Behind him, through an open window, are dark and billowing clouds above the ocean coast. This may refer to the Arundel's land in West Sussex along the southeast coast of England.

This print is one of over 100 from an edition of *Iconographia*. This was a series of portraits that, at Van Dyck's instigation, was first published between 1626 and 1635. It includes engravings and etchings of famous men, and some women, who achieved greatness as princes and nobles, statesmen and military leaders, or scholars and artists. Although some 20 prints were etched by Van Dyck in his signature sketchy style, the majority, like this print by Pierre Lombart, were engraved in a more traditional way.[3] KS

1   Arthur Wheelock, Susan Barnes and Julius Held, *Anthony Van Dyck, 1599-1641* (Washington: National Gallery of Art, c. 1990), 291-94. See also, Christopher White, *Anthony Van Dyck: Thomas Howard, The Earl of Arundel* (Malibu, CA: Getty Publications, 1995).

2   The portrait, dated to c. 1629-30, is currently in the Isabella Stewart Gardener Museum in Boston.

3   Ger Luijten, "The Iconography: Van Dyck's portraits in print," in Carl Depauw and Ger Luijten, *Anthony Van Dyck as a printmaker* (Amsterdam: Rijksmuseum, 1999), 72-91; and Arthur M. Hind, *Van Dyck, his Original Etchings and his Iconography* (Boston: Houghton Mifflin, 1915), 5-105. The print is not included in Marie Mauquoy-Hendrickx, *L'iconographie d'Antonie van Dyck: catalogue raisonné*, 2nd rev. ed., 2 vols. (Bruxelles : Bibliothèque Royale Albert I, 1991).

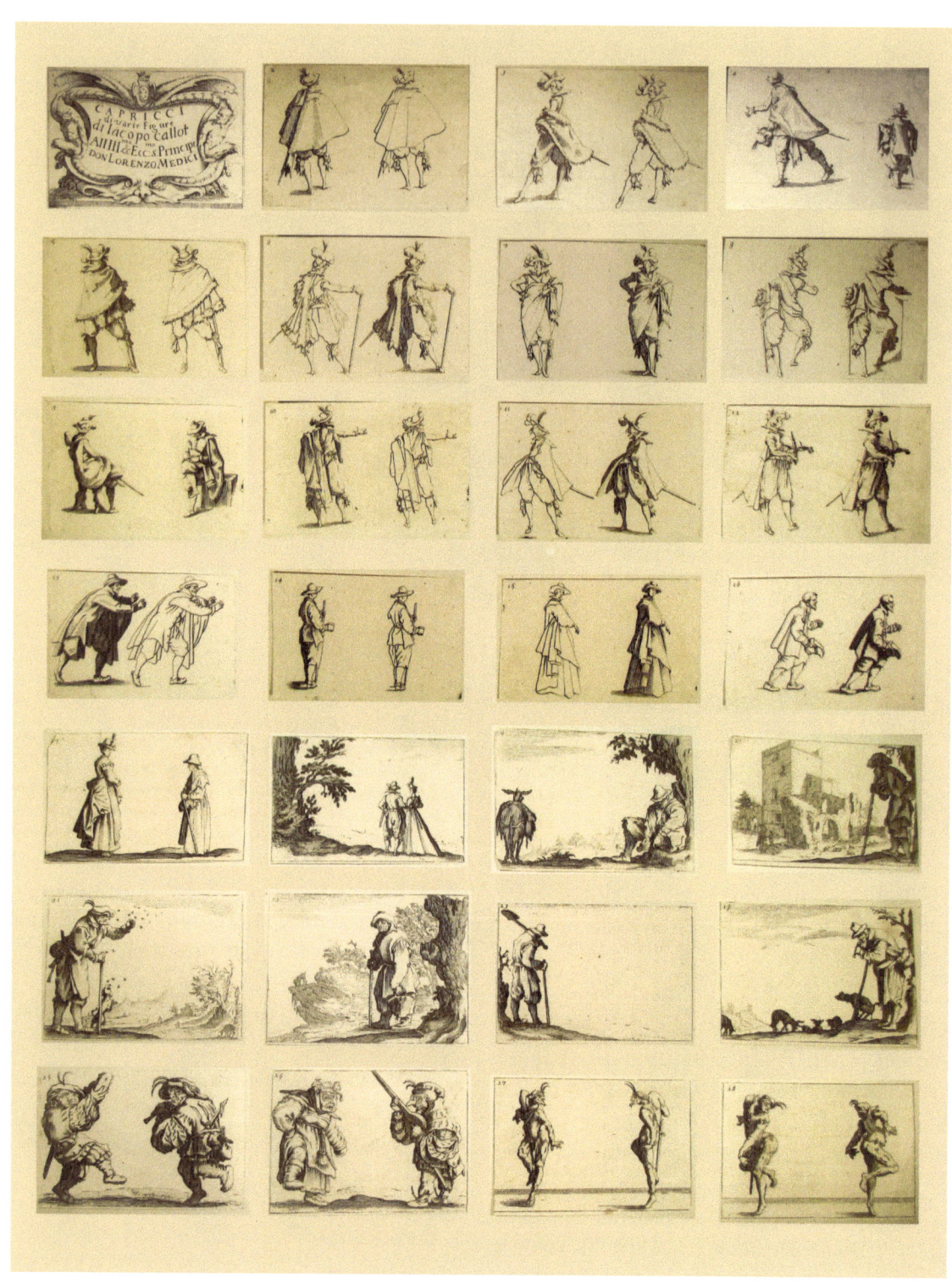

Cat. 11
Jacques Callot (1592-1635), French
From *Capricci di varie figure*, 1617 or 1623[1]
Etching
2 1/4" x 3 1/8" each
Gift of James T. Tanis and Dr. Justin Tanis
13-G-3586

Unlike many printmakers of the day, Callot came from a prosperous family, was familiar with court culture, and chose to study printmaking, which was then considered an artisanal craft. The breadth of his production and the innovation of his technique attest to his commitment to the medium.

As a young man, Callot traveled to Italy determined to study printmaking, and he remained there from 1609 until the early 1620s.[2] While in Florence, he was given an appointment in the court of the Medici. Among the many works he created for the court are the *Capricci*, or small whimsical images of different kinds of figures. A set was bound together and dedicated to the 17-year-old Prince Lorenzo, son of Grand Duke Cosimo II.[3] In them, Callot exhibits his powers of observation and his sense of humor.

In the main, the first three rows of prints illustrate noblemen. Callot humorously shows them in many poses and from many angles. Unexpected things jut out from the oddly-positioned figures. The viewers have to question what they are looking at. Is that a sword, an arm, a ribbon, a knee, or part of the cape? Where are the faces and the arms? Callot doubles the fun by illustrating these small figures twice in one print. He demonstrates how shading an outlined figure alters its appearance in significant ways. He showcases his innovative development of an etching process that used a hard varnish ground and a new type of etching needle, the échoppe, to give the printmaker greater flexibility and finesse in creating lines.[4]

Rows four and five contain depictions of peasants in the countryside. Since the mid-1500s, peasants in their environment had been a subject in art, and they appeared more frequently in the 17th century. The small size of the print did not deter Callot from including surprising details: a goat on a cliff, a defecating dog, a distant cityscape.

The bottom row contains prints of performers in 17th-century Florence. There are disfigured musicians, related to the *Gobbi* or dwarfs, who played at the court. There are also depictions of a dancing Pantaloon, the *commedia dell'arte* character known for his lechery and greed. The *commedia dell'arte* was a traveling street theater troupe popular at this time. The stock characters were set and recognizable to all by their costume—the scatter-brained professor, the heart-on-his-sleeve lover, the sassy flirt—but the plots were improvised on stage.[5]

Although Callot's *Capricci* images are fun-loving, some of his subject matter suggests a deep concern for the disadvantaged on the fringes of society, including beggars, gypsies, and victims of war. [6] EG

1   The *Capricci* were published first in Florence in 1617, and then after Callot's return to Nancy, France, in 1623. On his life, see Helen Diane Russell and Jeffrey Blanchard, *Jacques Callot: Prints and Related Drawings* (Washington, DC: National Gallery of Art, 1975), 3-17.

2   Howard Daniel, *Callot's Etchings* (New York: Dover, 1974), xi-xii.

3   Ibid., xii-xvi.

4   Ibid., xvi-xxii.

5   Gerald Kahn, *Jacques Callot: Artist of the Theater* (Athens: University of Georgia Press, 1976), 7-25, 91-94; and Donald Posner, "Jacques Callot and the Dances Called Sfessania," *The Art Bulletin* 59, no. 2 (1977): 203-216.

6   Russell and Blanchard, *Jacques Callot*, 48-56, 209-269.

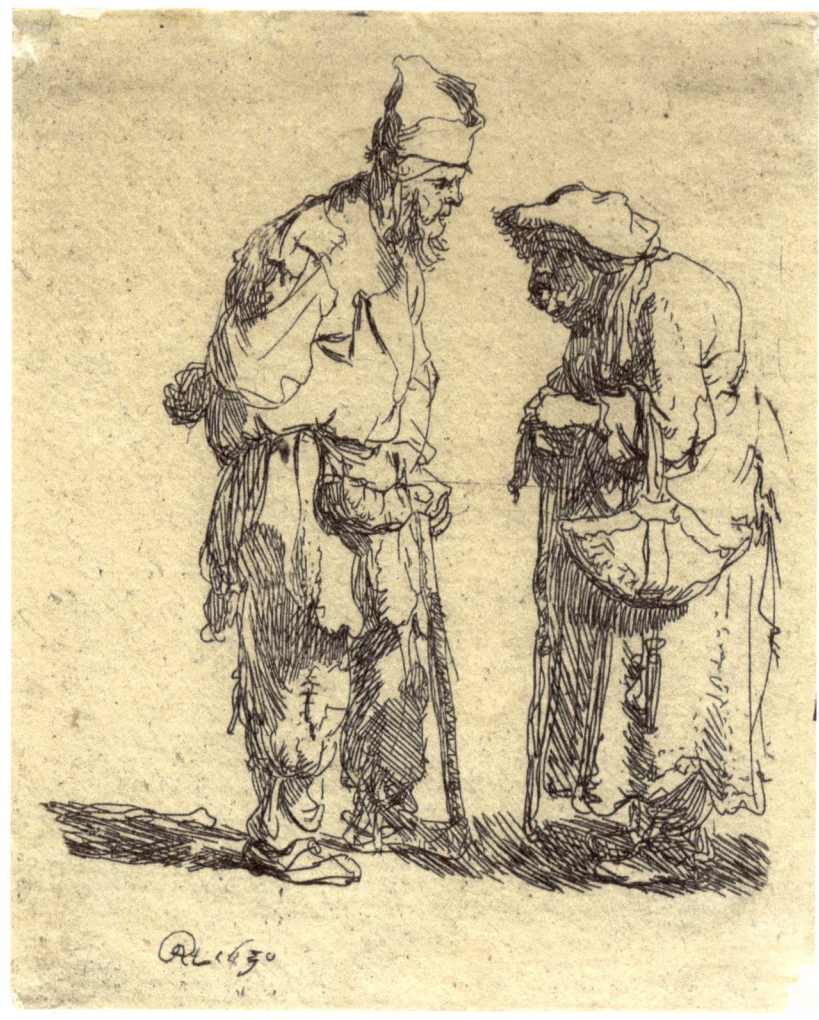

Cat. 12
Rembrandt van Rijn (1606-1669), Dutch
Beggar Man and Woman Conversing, 1630
2 ⁵/₈" x 2"
Etching
96-G-3200
Gift of Mr. and Mrs. Jay Stiefel

The elderly man and woman, dressed in ragged clothes, interact in a civil manner with one another. The satchel around his waist and the basket on her arm suggest that despite their poverty, they have a place in the economy of 17th-century Netherlands.

Impoverished peasants were popular subjects in the 17th century. But beggars, society's marginalized citizens, were less frequently represented in art. Attitudes towards social outcasts in the Protestant Dutch society were complex. The good beggar was one who was the recipient of generous community charity. Different from the roaming vagrant, he/she was known to a commu-nity, but was expected to be invisible to it. In the early 1630s, Rembrandt van Rijn, who came to be known just as Rembrandt, illustrated them in a compassionate way.[1] The artist may have identified with beggars because, throughout was life, he was anxious about his finances.[2]
IM, KS

1   Robert Baldwin, "'On earth we are beggars, as Christ himself was': The Protestant Background of Rembrandt's Imagery of Poverty, Disability, and Begging," *Konsthistorisk Tidskrift* 56, no. 3 (1985): 122-135; and Simon Schama, *Rembrandt's Eyes* (New York: Alfred A. Knopf, 1999), 303-307. Schama illustrates Rembrandt's etched *Self-Portrait as a Beggar*.

2   Gary Schwartz, *Rembrandt's Universe: his life, his art, his world* (London: Thames and Hudson, 2006); Paul Crenshaw, *Rembrandt's Bankruptcy: The Artist, His Patrons, and the Art World in Seventeenth-Century Netherlands* (Cambridge: Cambridge University Press, 2006); and Svetlana Alpers, *Rembrandt's Enterprise: The Studio and the Market* (Chicago: University of Chicago Press, 1988), 88-122.

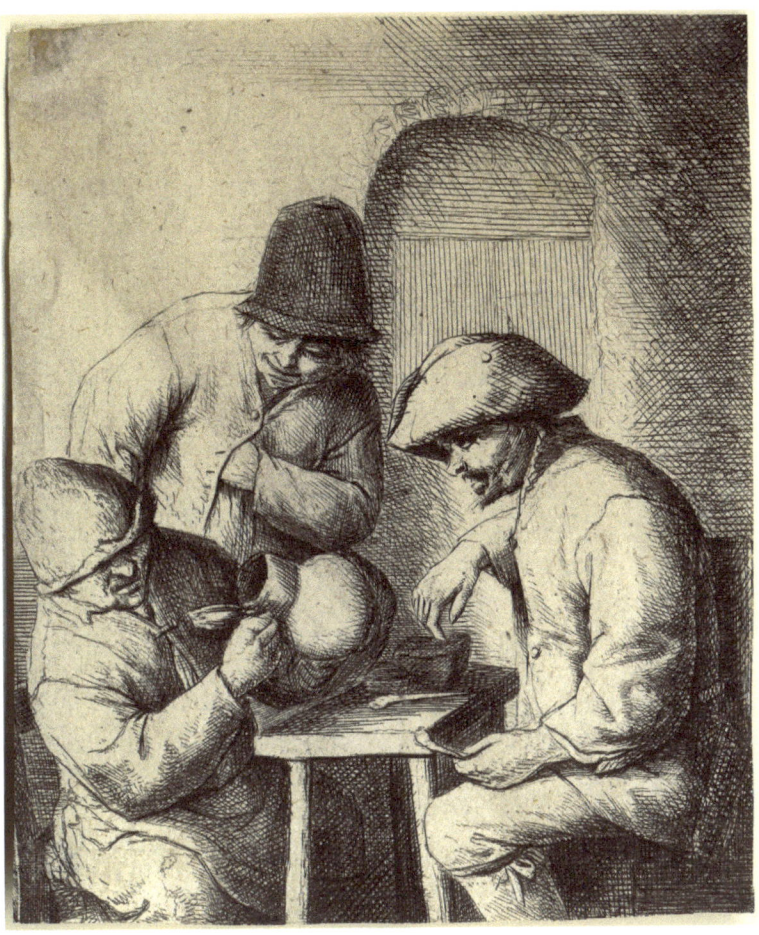

Cat. 13
Adriaen van Ostade (1610-1685), Dutch
The Empty Jug, c. 1653
4" x 3 3/8"
Etching
81-G-1133

Two men react as their companion looks disgruntledly into an empty beer tankard. The standing man reaches into his jacket, perhaps in search of coins to pay for a refill. The seated one looks on with interest as he fills his pipe.

Van Ostade captures the realities of 17th-century Dutch country folk. In this sparse setting, around a small table next to a boarded window, perhaps in an inn, the men gather to drink and smoke. Some critics read this depiction of peasants, with their odd-shaped hats, as ridiculing.[1] Others see it as sympathetic, capturing the companionship of men after their hard labors.[2] HM

1   Louis Godefroy, *The Complete Etchings of Adriaen Van Ostade*, originally published 1930, reprint (San Francisco: Alan Wofsy Fine Arts, 1990), 15.

2   Anna C. Knaap, "From Lowlife to Rustic Idyll: the Peasant Genre in 17th-Century Dutch Drawings and Prints," *Harvard University Art Museums Bulletin* 4, no. 2 (spring 1996): 31-33, 42-47. Knaap argues that even as the circumstances for peasants changed in 17th-century Netherlands, with some becoming more financially stable and underwritten by the urban economy and others becoming less financially stable and more migratory in their search for work, very few artists distinguished pictorially between peasants in those various circumstances.

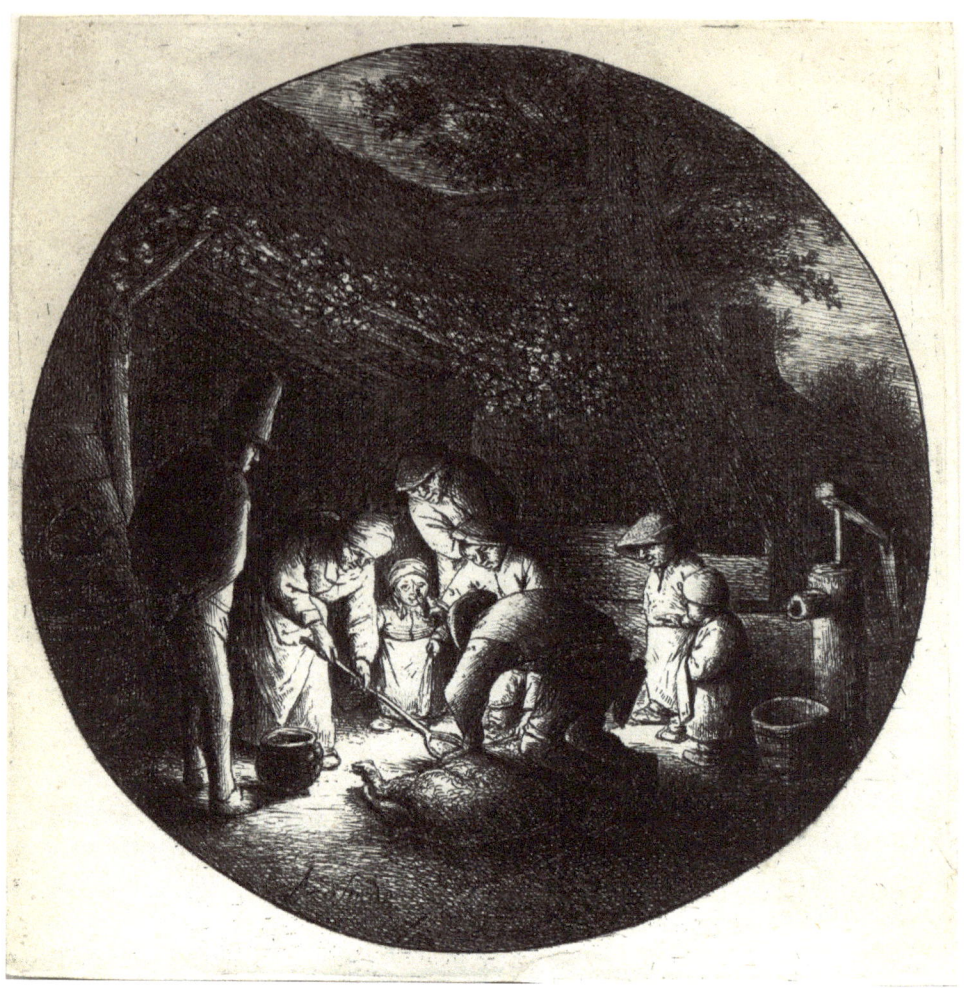

Cat. 14
Adriaen van Ostade (1610 -1685), Dutch
The Pig Killers, c. 1642
4 ³/₄" diameter
Etching
13-G-3583
Gift of James T. Tanis and Dr. Justin Tanis

Van Ostade is best known for his portrayal of country life—a popular subject among collectors in the Dutch cities. Here we see a family gathered outside their humble home, witnessing and helping to slaughter a pig. Some are engrossed with working on the animal's carcass, and others are smiling because the flesh and blood will feed them throughout the winter. The light source comes from a hidden lantern near the pig, which casts striking shadows on the figures. [1]

This scene likely represents the month of November. Since medieval times, images of specific activities that happened throughout the year would appear sculpted in 12 roundels around cathedral portals to remind viewers of the passage of earthly time as part of God's creation. [2] This print is reminiscent of the imagery in those roundels. KS, MD

1   Linda C. Hults, *The Print in the Western World: an Introductory History* (Madison: University of Wisconsin Press, 1996), 222. See also Clifford Ackley, ed., *Printmaking in the Age of Rembrandt* (Boston: Museum of Fine Arts, 1981), 157-159, 161-162.

2   Peter van der Coelen, Theo Laurentius, S. William Pelletier, Tom Rassieur, and Leonard J. Slatkes, *Everyday Life in Hollands's Golden Age: The Complete Etchings of Adriaen van Ostade* (Amsterdam: Museum Het Rembrandthuis, 1998), 145-146. This interpretation is not universally accepted. On medieval cathedral decoration of the labors of the months, see Michael Camille, *Gothic Art, Glorious Visions* (New York: Harry N. Abrams, 1996), 95-97.

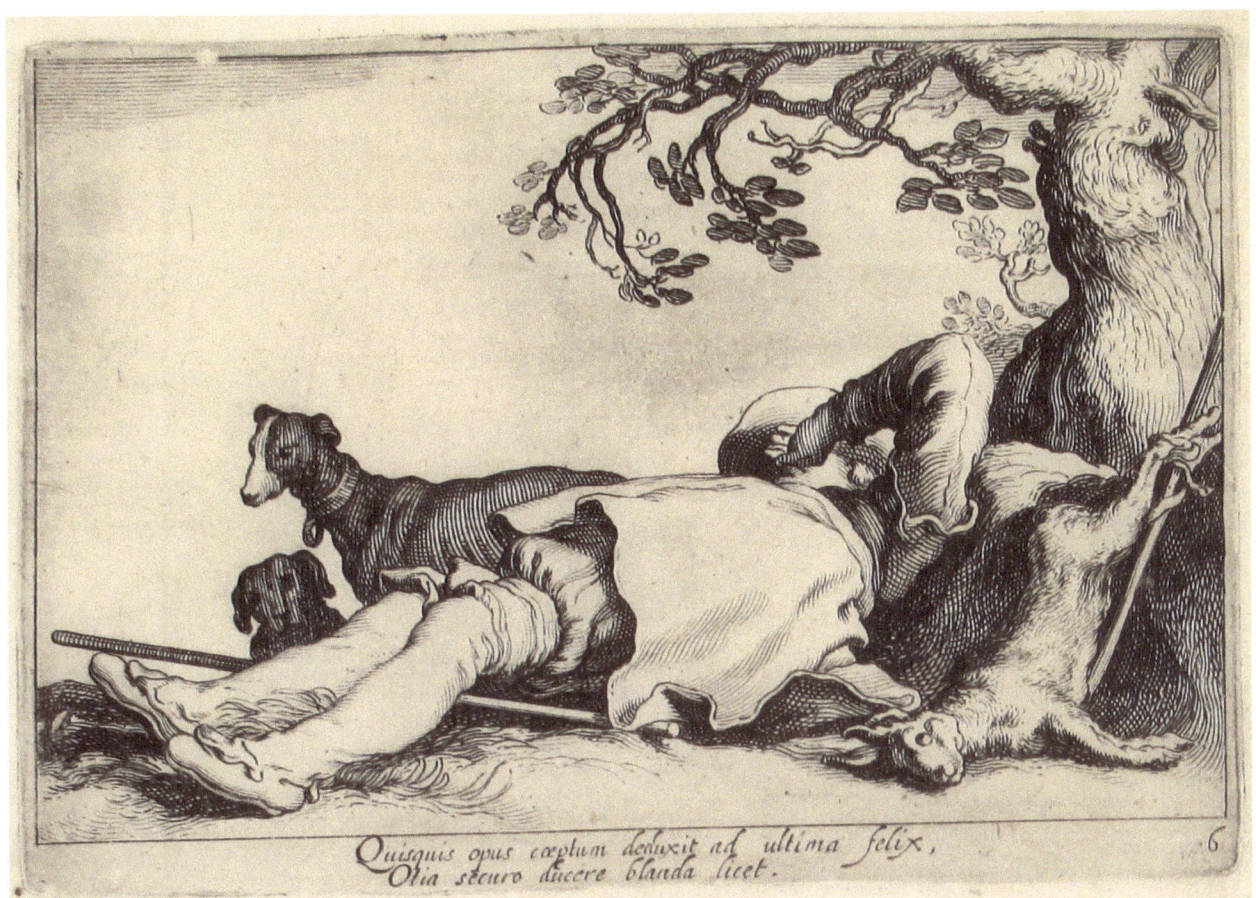

Quisquis opus coeptum deduxit ad ultima felix,
Otia securo ducere blanda licet.

Cat. 15
Cornelis Bloemaert II (1603- c. 1684), Dutch
After Abraham Bloemaert (1566-1651), Dutch
A Hunter Resting by a Tree, c. 1626
From the series *Otia Delectant*
4 3/16" x 6"
Etching
90-G-3071

This print is one of a series of 16 images, representing various people from the countryside—farmers, hunters, peddlars, and soldiers—taking pleasure in resting after their labors. Abraham Bloemaert conceived the series around 1620-25, and most of the prints were engraved by his son Cornelius soon thereafter.[1] The series is unique in the 17th century in that it promotes a "new qualified approach to work and to rest."[2] Here rest is not a vice but rather it is something to be enjoyed by those who work earnestly, honestly and piously.

This print illustrates a hunter's reward after accomplishing his goal. The hunter lies on his back under a tree, napping with his hand over his eyes. His two dogs are by his side, watching over their master and the results of the hunt, the large hare. The inscription translates as: "Happy who completes work which he started; he is entitled to enjoy leisure safely.[3] KS

1   On Abraham Bloemaert, see Marcel Röthlisberg, *Abraham Bloemaert and his sons: paintings and prints* (Doornspijk: Davaco, 1993), v. 1, 15-19; on Cornelis Bloemaert, see Ibid., v. 1, 513-14. Another less well-known son Frederick engraved four of the 16 prints.

2   Ibid., v. 1, 33.

3   Ibid., v. 1, 231-33; v. 2, fig. 439 (cat. 302).

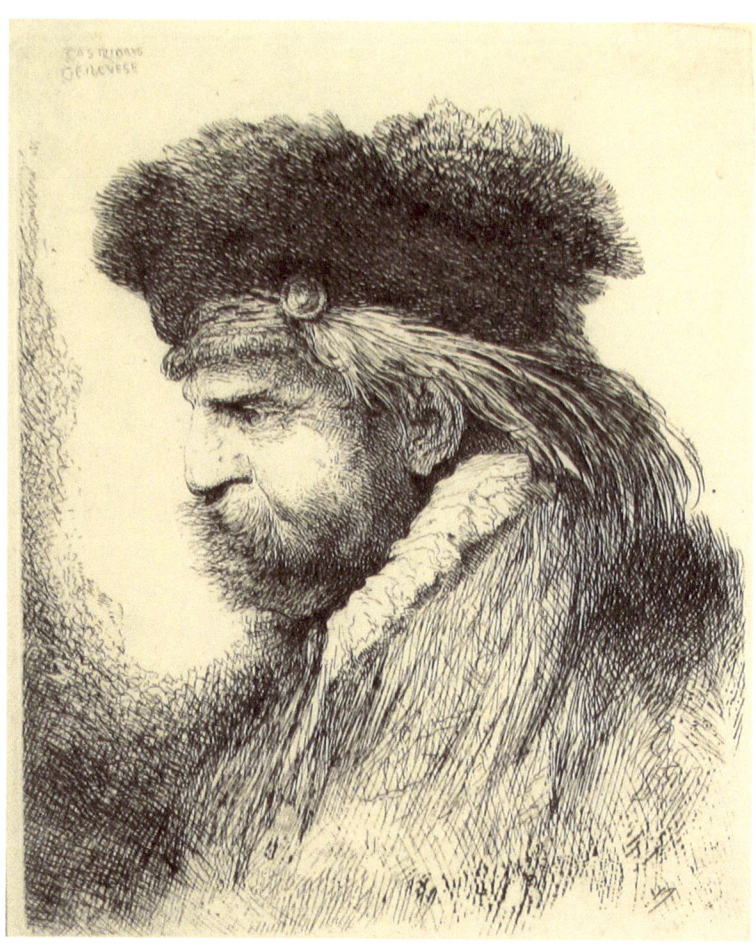

Cat. 16
Giovanni Benedetto Castiglione (1609-1664), Italian
Head of Man with a Moustache, Wearing a Fur Headdress, Facing Left, mid- to late 1640s
5 ⅝" x 4 ⁹⁄₁₆"
Etching
82-G-1211

Castiglione depicts a man with a grand mustache and bristly whiskers. He sports a fur cap with a side plume held in place by a medallion, and a lace collar. The image is one in a series of prints of character heads with exotic costumes and exaggerated features. Known as "tronies", these heads were popular in Dutch Baroque society. Rembrandt was well known for producing many such heads, and Castiglione embraces the trend here.[1]

Castiglione's depictions were not intended to be authentic portraits, but rather to demonstrate the artist's inventiveness.[2] Nonetheless, they suggest a cultural interest in people from different parts of the world, in this case Eastern Europe or Russia. Merchants, dignitaries, immigrants, refugees and slaves from the East would have been familiar sights in Italy, and Italian merchants and travelers returned with stories about other cultures. HM, RC

1   Timothy J. Standring and Martin Clayton, *Castiglione: Lost Genius* (London: Royal Collection Trust, 2013), 81. Castiglione did two series, one with images of about 180 x 130 mm, and another of about 140 x 115 mm. This print is from the small series.

2   For more on Castiglione's life and his technical innovations, see essay in this catalogue by Rachel Christie.

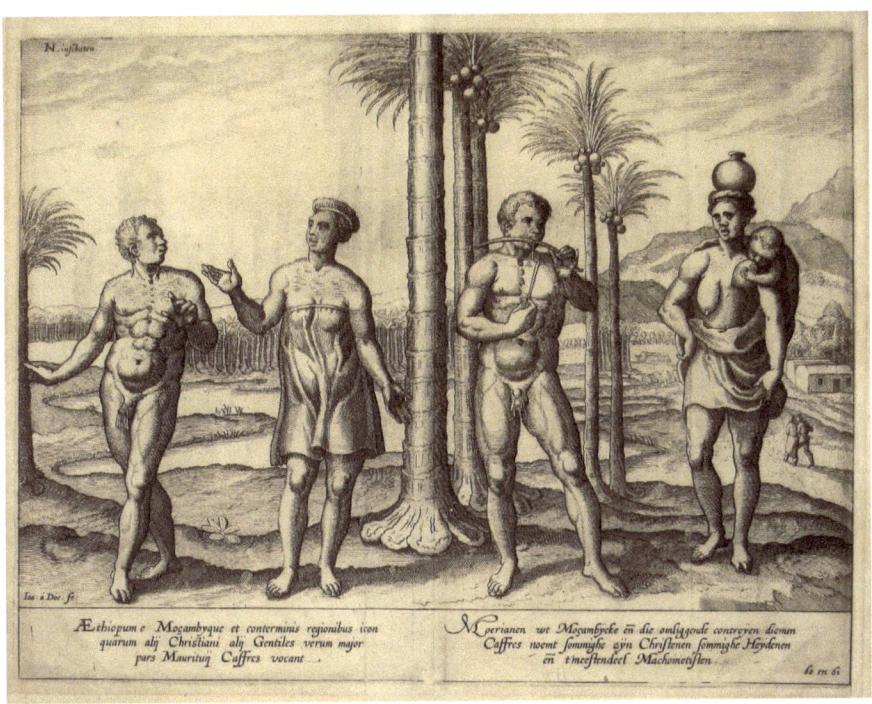

Cat. 17
Jan van Doetechum, the Younger (c. 1560-1630), Dutch
After drawing by Jan Huygen van Linschoten (1563-1611), Dutch
Christian and Muslim Couple from Mozambique, from Jan Huygen van Linschoten, *Itinerario* (Amsterdam, 1596)
10 3/8" x 8 3/16"
Engraving
96-G-3199
Gift of Mr. and Mrs. Jay Stiefel

Van Linschoten was a Dutch merchant who published an influential book on his travels to the East Indies, i.e., South and Southeast Asia.[1] His journey to this part of the world required sailing along the coastline of Africa, and he recorded his observations of the people and the land in both word and image. Van Linschoten did not draw the illustrations on site, and they are not authentic representations. Rather they were intended to give his readers a rough indication of the Mozambicans. They are depicted with idealized bodies posed in classical stances, but also with stereotypical African features.[2]

According to the text at the bottom of the print, the scantily-clad couple on the right is Catholic, having been converted by Portuguese missionaries. The other naked couple is Muslim. Europeans, and particularly the Protestant Dutch, believed that nonchalance about nudity and about caring for children—suckling them without cradling them—was indicative of an uncultured

people.[3] The image implies that that conversion to Catholicism or to Islam did not ensure the attainment of good mores.

The illustration points to an interest in, but no real understanding of, other cultures encountered by traveling Europeans. For many decades, this print was reproduced in travel books and did much to engrain prejudices about East Africans. SD

1 Jan Huygen van Linschoten, *Itinerario: Voyage ofte schipvaert van Jan Huyghen van Linschoten naer Oost ofte Portugaels Indien* (Amsterdam: Cornelis Claesz, 1596). In it, he identified a sea route through the Straits of Malacca, near Malaysia, and thus encouraged Northern European travelers and merchants on the way to the Far East to bypass lands held by the Portuguese. As the voyage circumnavigated the coast of Africa, he provided descriptions of the lands and peoples of Africa. The book was popular among Northern Europeans and was re-issued many times and translated very quickly into English, German, Latin and French.

2 Ernst van den Boogaart, "De Brys' Africa," in Susanna Burghartz, ed., *Inszenierte Welten: Die west und ostindischen Reisen der Verleger de Bry, 1590-1630* (Basel: Schwabe, 2004), 95-155. I would like to thank Prof. Michael McInneshin, La Salle University History Department, for his help in locating this source.

3 Ibid., 109-118.

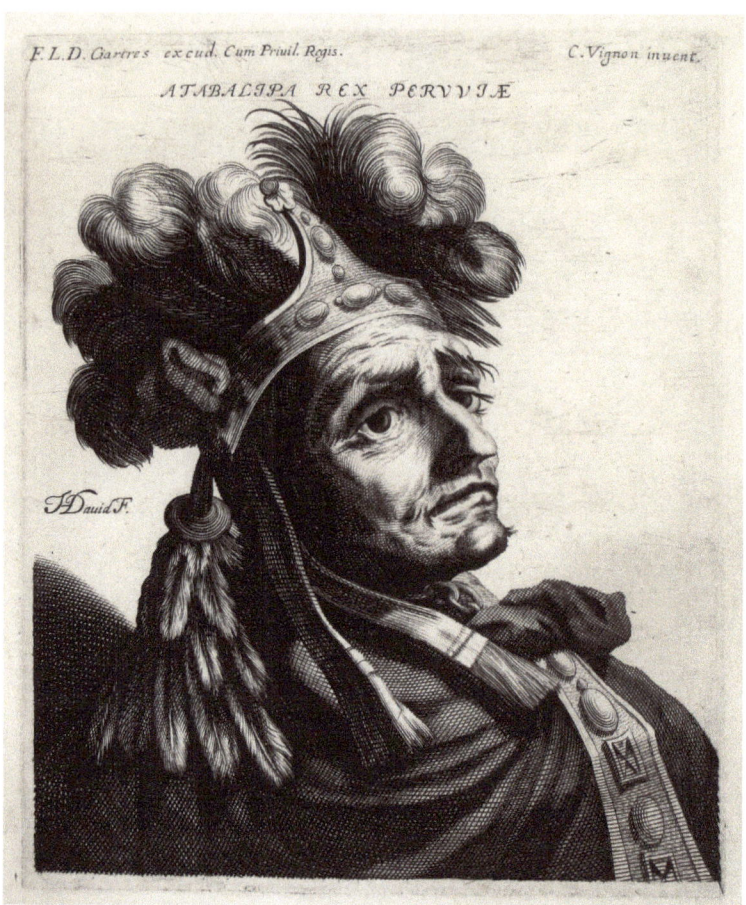

F.L.D. Gartres excud. Cum Priuil. Regis.   C. Vignon inuent.

ATABALIPA REX PERVVIÆ

Cat. 18
Attributed to Jérôme David (1600-1670), French
After drawing by Claude Vignon (1633-1703), French
Published by François Langlois (alias Ciartres)
Atahualpa, Incan Emperor
From the series *Bustes Philosophes et de Rois*, 1635
8 ¾" x 7 ¼"
Engraving
13-G-3550

Atahualpa was the last Sapa Inca (all-powerful emperor) to rule over the mighty Inca Empire (present-day Peru, Ecuador, Bolivia, Colombia and Chile). His death in 1533 marked the end of the Inca Empire and the beginning of Spanish colonization in South America.[1] It is highly unlikely that the artist had ever seen a portrait of the emperor, and he represented Atahualpa in an idealized and romanticized manner. Atahualpa looks resignedly over his right shoulder. He wears an elaborate feathered headdress only loosely-based on those recorded by 16th-century Spanish and Incans. Although gold often formed the base of the crown, here the front piece is bejeweled in a European manner. The ostrich feathers in the crown were fashionable in 17th-century France.

This print is one of 36 illustrations, many of which depicted historical non-European leaders who were defeated by Europeans. Their demise marked the expansion of European power. They include the Patagonian chief Paracoussi, the Ottoman sultan Saladin, and the Algerian pasha Hayreddin.[2] The prints' issue in 1635, at a time when France was creating colonial territories in the Caribbean, suggests a misguided curiosity and exoticized view of other cultures. KS

1   Kim MacQuarrie, *The Last Days of the Incans* (New York: Simon and Schuster, 2007), 69-137. We extend thanks to Prof. Mey-Yen Moriuchi for her special assistance in constructing this label.

2   Paola Bassani, *Claude Vignon, 1593-1670* (Paris: Arthena, 1992), 283-95. Of the 36 prints in the series, 24 were after designs by Claude Vignon.

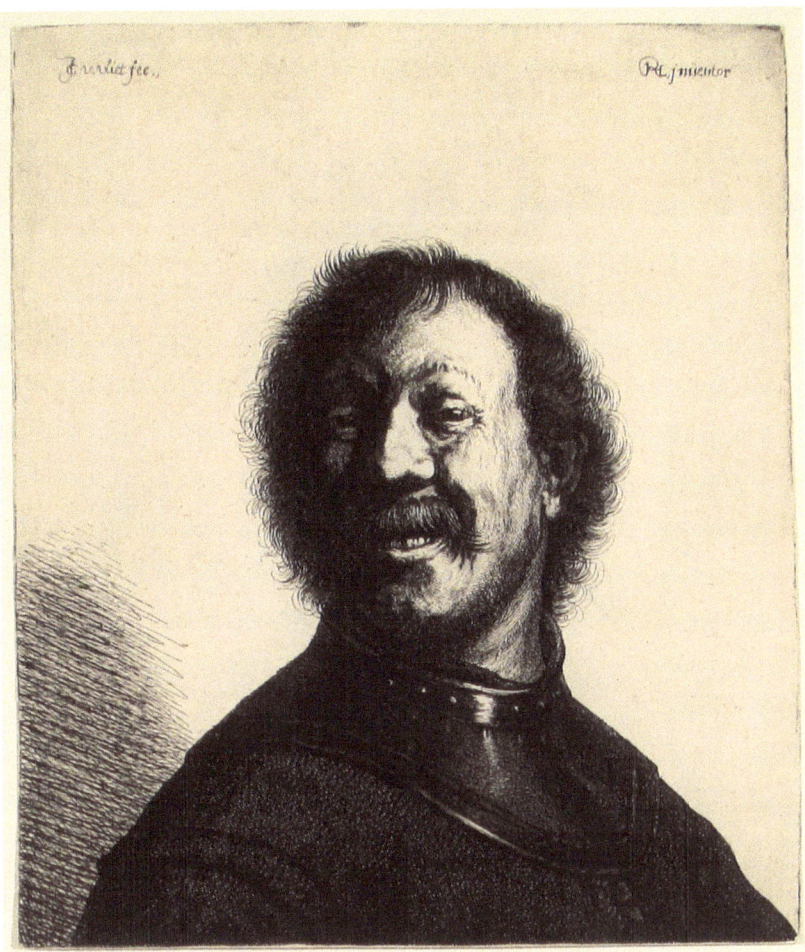

Cat. 19
Jan Georg van Vliet (c. 1610-c. 1635), Dutch
After a lost painting by Rembrandt van Rijn, c. 1627-28
Laughing Man in a Gorget, c. 1634
10 9/16" x 8 3/8"
Etching
70-G-296

The man wears a gorget, a metal breastplate with a collar that functions as armor. Van Vliet's portrayal is much like that of the laughing cavalier, or a mounted soldier of a high rank. The cavalier was popular subject in the 17th century. At the time, there was concern about returning or off-duty soldiers in civil society. In paintings and prints of the day, the soldier is shown as possessing a devil-may-care attitude. He drinks too much, smokes too much, loses at card games, cheats at card games, seduces local girls, and visits brothels.[1] Van Vliet's soldier, caught in a spontaneous mid-laugh, conveys something of this attitude. The manic expression might also elicit some anxiety from the 17th-century viewer. The mysterious shadow serves to deepen that anxiety.

The print is one of a series of "tronies" popular in the Baroque period. Van Vliet used a now-lost painted self-portrait of Rembrandt in costume as a model for the head.[2] After this figure was paired with another of Van Vliet's heads, that of a grieving man, the two earned the title of the Laughing Democritus and the Weeping Heraclitus, two ancient Greek philosophers.[3] KS

1   Jochai Rosen, *Soldiers at Leisure: the Guardroom Scene in Dutch Genre Painting of the Golden Age* (Amsterdam: Amsterdam University Press, 2010).

2   Van Vliet is known as Rembrandt's printmaker because many of his works reproduce Rembrandt's paintings or show some intervention by Rembrandt. On his life, see Christiaan Schuckman, Martin Royalton-Kisch, and Erick Hinterding, *Rembrandt and Van Vliet: A Collaboration on Copper* (Amsterdam: Museum Het Rembrandthuis, 1996), 8-14.

3   Ibid., 50-65. On Rembrandt's painting, see H. Perry Chapman, *Rembrandt's Self-Portraits: A Study in Seventeenth-Century Identity* (Princeton: Princton University Press, 1990), 38-40.

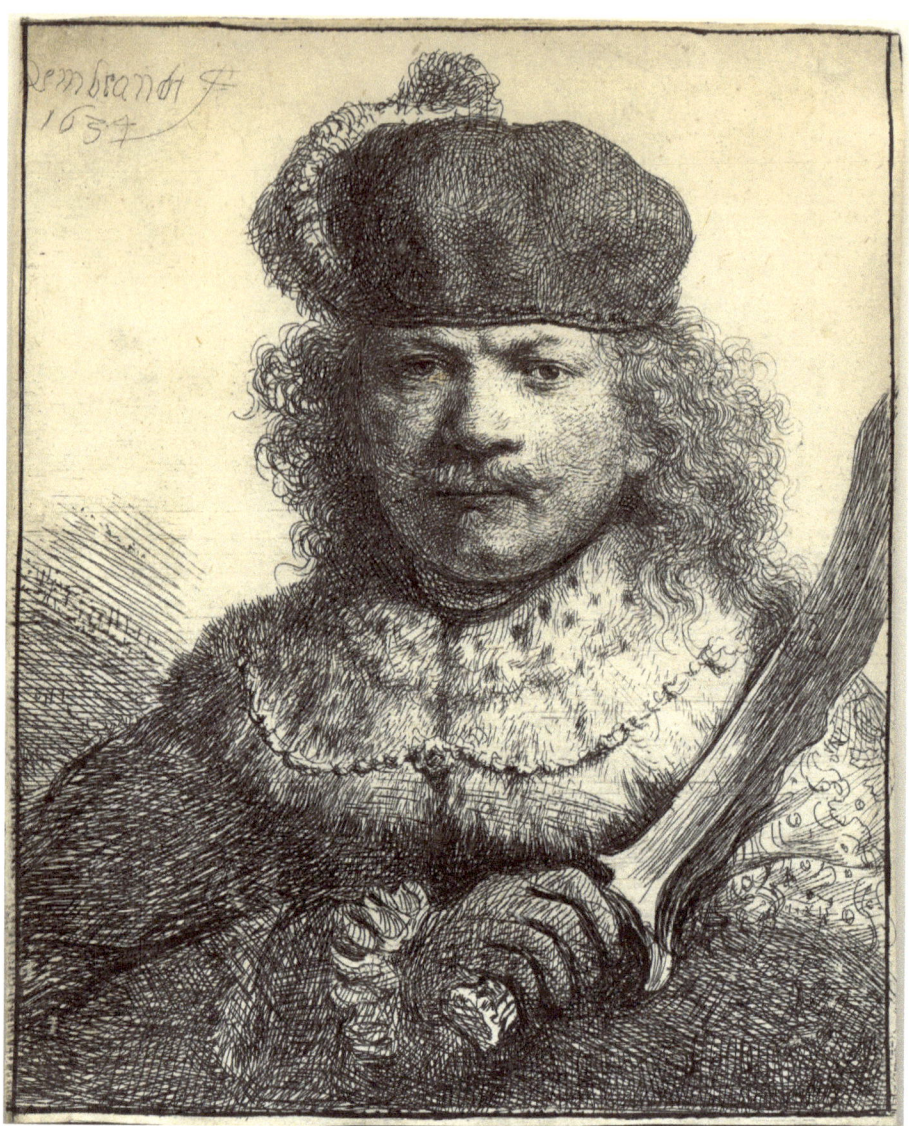

Cat. 20
Rembrandt van Rijn (1606-1669), Dutch
Self-Portrait with Raised Saber, 1634
Etching
4 13/16" x 4"
76-G-596

Over the course of his life, Rembrandt produced over 70 self-portraits in both paintings and etchings. While artists' self-portraits were common in 17th-century Netherlands, the number and variety of Rembrandt's set him apart from his fellow artists. As with many of his self-portraits before 1648, Rembrandt is dressed in a costume. Rembrandt was an avid collector of fanciful paraphernalia, which he kept in his studio for costuming models, including himself. His identities included a courtier, a beggar, a soldier and a saint. Here he has donned an ermine stole and a crown, and regally raises a saber as he stares authoritatively at the viewer. Recent scholars have understood these self-portraits not as expressions of a complex inner life, but as strategies to establish his identity and to distinguish himself as an artist. [1] KS

1   H. Perry Chapman, *Rembrandt's Self-Portraits, A Study in Seventeenth-Century Identity* (Princeton: Princeton University Press, 1990), 34-36, 43.

Light

The manipulation of light and shadow to create a sense of intrigue is one of the major hallmarks of Baroque art. The Italian painter Caravaggio best represents this tendency. His use of an extreme form of chiaroscuro—a word combination meaning light/dark—called tenebrism (the dark manner) put great swaths of the painted canvas in near darkness, while others were glaringly lit. The effect is that the viewer is absorbed, and sometimes put on edge or confused, by what is only partially revealed.

Sometimes in Baroque imagery, the light emanates from a single source, one internal to the image. The moon, a hand-held torch, or even the halo of a divine being, throws light in limited and directed ways. In other cases, light streams from an unseen window or door located just beyond the image frame. Shadows are predictable, falling on areas or surfaces far from the light. In spotlighting, the Baroque artist used multiple light sources as an alternative way to create drama. The play of light and shadow is irrational, even chaotic. The result is a high-energy composition across whose surface the viewer's eye dances.

The medium of printmaking provided ample opportunity for artists of the Baroque to produces patches of light and shadow. In engraving—inscribing a metal plate with a design using a metal tool called a burin, and then inking the plate and printing it—shadows are generally created by cross-hatching, a weave of straight lines, mainly consistent in width. In etching—using acid rather than a burin to dig into the metal plate—shadows could be more creatively and variably created. Generally, the etched line is more fluid and fluctuating in width. In addition, during the inking process, some artists could produce velvety patches of black on the paper by varying the amount of ink wiped from the plate before printing. SD

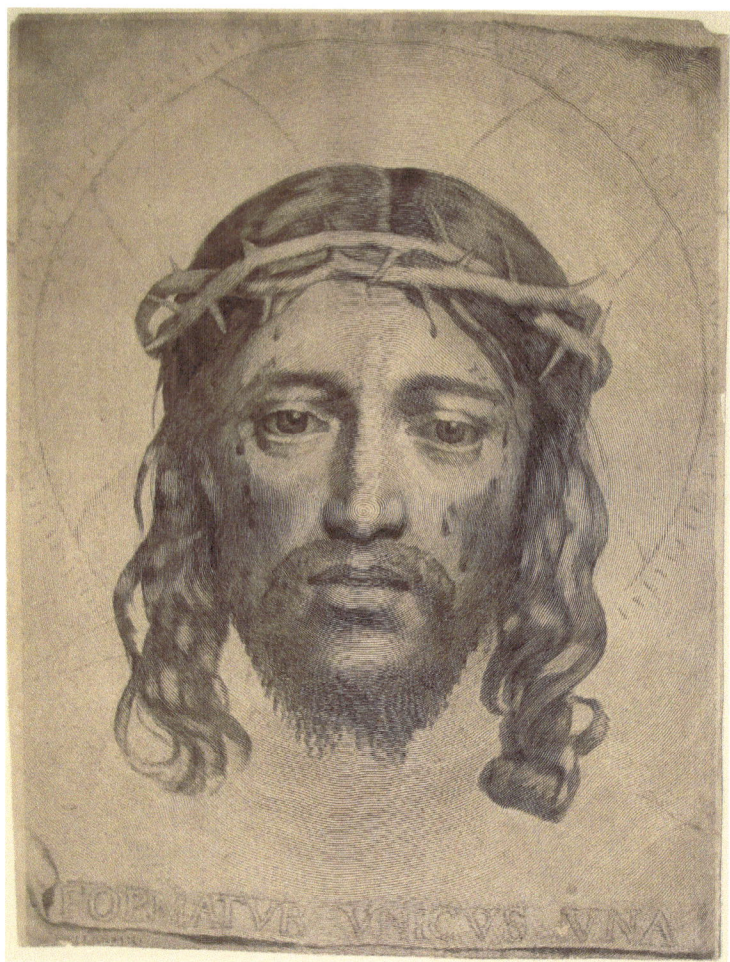

Cat. 21
Claude Mellan (1598-1688), French
The Sudarium, or *The Veil of St. Veronica*, 1649
16 ⁷/₈" x 12 ³/₈"
Engraving
69-G-257

Mellan developed a distinct manner of engraving. To the delight of art critics, he defined forms using mainly parallel lines, with no outline and minimal crosshatching. Some lauded his ability to mesmerize viewers who are compelled to scrutinize the lines on the surface of the print even as the form eludes them in the process.[1] The avid print collector and connoisseur Michel de Marolles, the Abate of Villeloin, gave the artist the idea for this celebrated print of the Sudarium. With one line, beginning at the center of the composition on the tip of Christ's nose and spiraling outward, the printmaker created the image of the impression made by Christ's face on St. Veronica's veil, providing what is thought to be

His only authentic portrait.

The inscription "Formatur unicus una, non alter" informs us that the composition was completed with one line, and dares others to replicate it. Mellan's biographer Pierre Mariette states that others did try but failed.[2] IM, SD

1   For his life and work, see Luigi Ficacci, *Claude Mellan, gli anni romani. Un incisore tra Vouet e Bernini* (Rome: Multigrafica Editrice, 1989); and Maxime Préaud and Barbara Brejon de Lavergnée, *L'Oiel d'or: Claude Mellan 1598-1688* (Paris: Bibliothèque nationale, 1988). For the response of some art critics, see Rebecca Zorbach, "'A secret kind of charm not to be explained or discerned': On Claude Millan's Insinuating Line," *RES: Anthropology and Aesthetics 5/6: Absconding* (spring/autumn 2009): 235-51.

2   Ficacci, *Claude Mellan, gli anni romani*, 60.

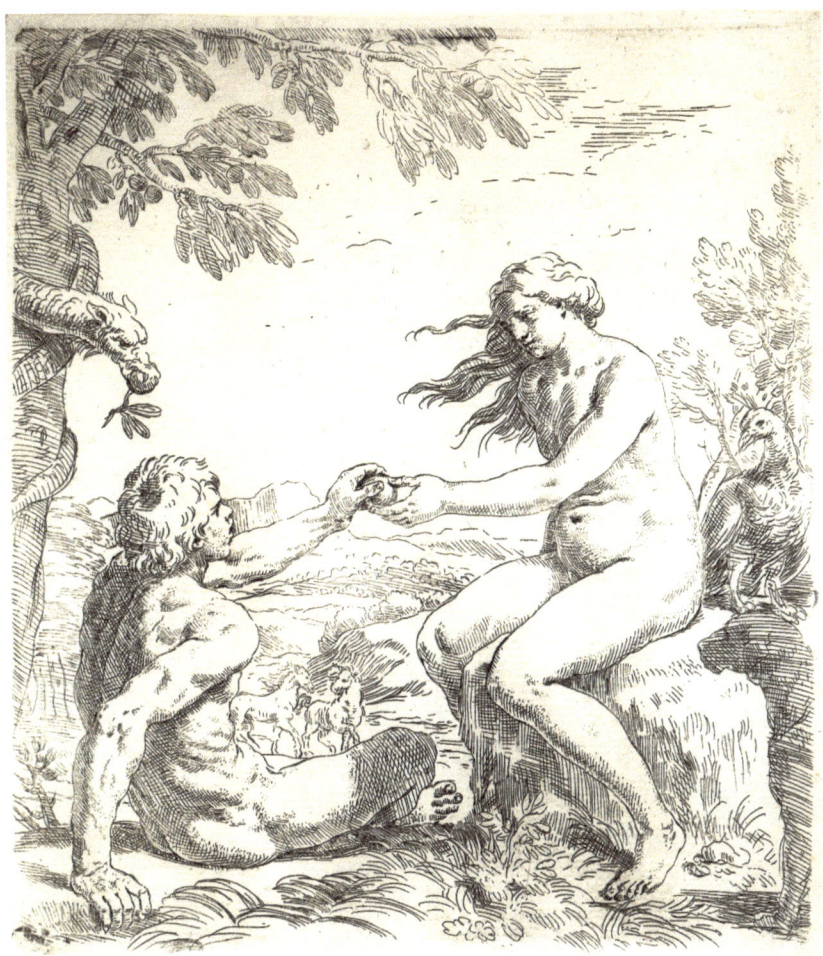

Cat. 22
Simone Cantarini (1612-1648), Italian
Adam and Eve, c. 1639
7 ³/₄" x 6 ⁷/₈"
Etching
79-G-1031

Primarily a painter, Cantarini created 37 etchings over the course of his career.[1] This print of Eve handing Adam the apple likely dates to a time when he worked briefly for the Duke of Mantua, Carlo II Gonzaga di Nevers.[2] The horses in the center background and the dog in the right foreground allude to the Gonzaga family's famed love of these animals. The eagle that sits behind Eve is a feature of the Gonzaga coat-of-arms. The dragon-headed snake might refer to the city of Mantua with its renowned Castle of St. George, named after the medieval saint who slaughtered a dragon to save a princess. The creatures in the print suggest that the city was much like the Garden of Eden.

Cantarini's efforts at flattering his patron might not have been appreciated. His biographer tells us that Cantarini became ill and died shortly after Duke Carlo II criticized the artist's work.[3] CA

1   Sue Welsh Reed and Richard Wallace, *Italian Etchers of the Renaissance and Baroque* (Boston: Museum of Fine Arts, 1989), 128-130, and Paolo Bellini, *L'opera incise di Simone Cantarini* (Milan: Comune di Milano, Ripartizione cultura e spettacolo, 1980), 18.

2   Kate Simone, *Renaissance Tapestry: the Gonzaga of Mantua* (New York: Harper and Row, 1988), 275-79.

3   There is reason to doubt this. Cantarini's two biographers recount different stories about his death at an early age. See Filippo Baldinucci, *Notizie dei professori deil disegno, originally published 1681-1728*, eds. Paola Barocchi and Antonio Boschetto (Florence, S.P.E.S., 1974), iv, 40–49; and Carlo Cesare Malvasia, *Felsina pittrice: vite dei pittori bolognesi*, originally published 1678, ed. Marcella Brascaglia (Bologna: ALFA, 1971), 587–601.

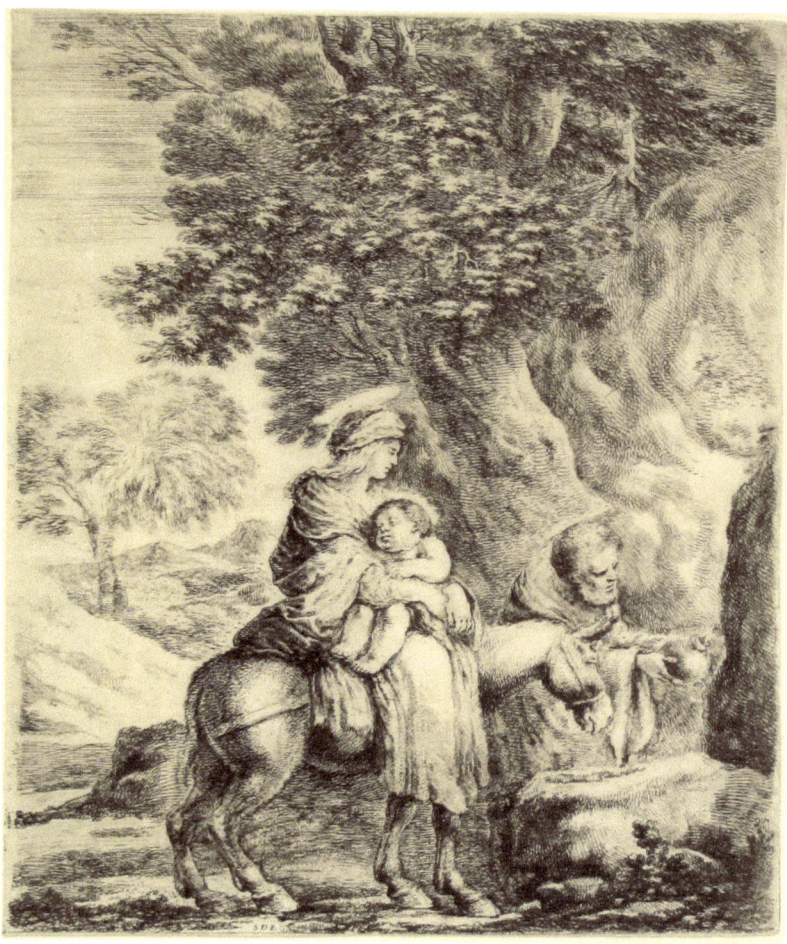

Cat. 23
Stefano della Bella (1610-1664), Italian
Flight into Egypt, 1652
5 $\frac{13}{16}$" x 4 $\frac{13}{16}$"
Etching
70-G-295

Della Bella was an assiduous and dedicated printmaker, better known for capturing contemporary events, such as military battle and theatrical performances, than for his religious subjects. However, of the religious prints, he created quite a few versions of the Flight into Egypt. In this one, Joseph leads Mary and the sleeping Christ Child on a donkey as they escape Herod's threat to kill the baby. He stops to place a jug under a spring that miraculously flows from a rock.[1] The Flight into Egypt is not well narrated in the Gospel. Rather, the detail about the miraculous spring derives from biblical Apocrypha. The scene persisted in the visual arts because it humanized the biblical characters for the faithful.[2] It also em-phasized Christ's identification with Moses, who fled out of Egypt in *Exodus* and who miraculously drew water from a rock.

By the 1650s, della Bella's style was heavily influenced by Jacques Callot.[3] His etched lines are feathery and create a silvery light around the figures. TC

1   Alessandro Baudi di Vesme and Phyllis Dearborn Massar, *Stefano della Bella, catalogue raisonné* (New York: Collectors Edition, 1971), vol. 1, 47 and vol. 2, 14II/II.

2   Gertrud Schiller, *Iconography of Christian Art* (New York: New York Graphic Society, 1971), vol. 1, 117-123.

3   Phyllis Dearborn Massar, *Presenting Stefano dell a Bella: Seventeenth-Century Print-maker* (New York: Metropolitan Museum of Art, 1971), 7-10, 27-35.

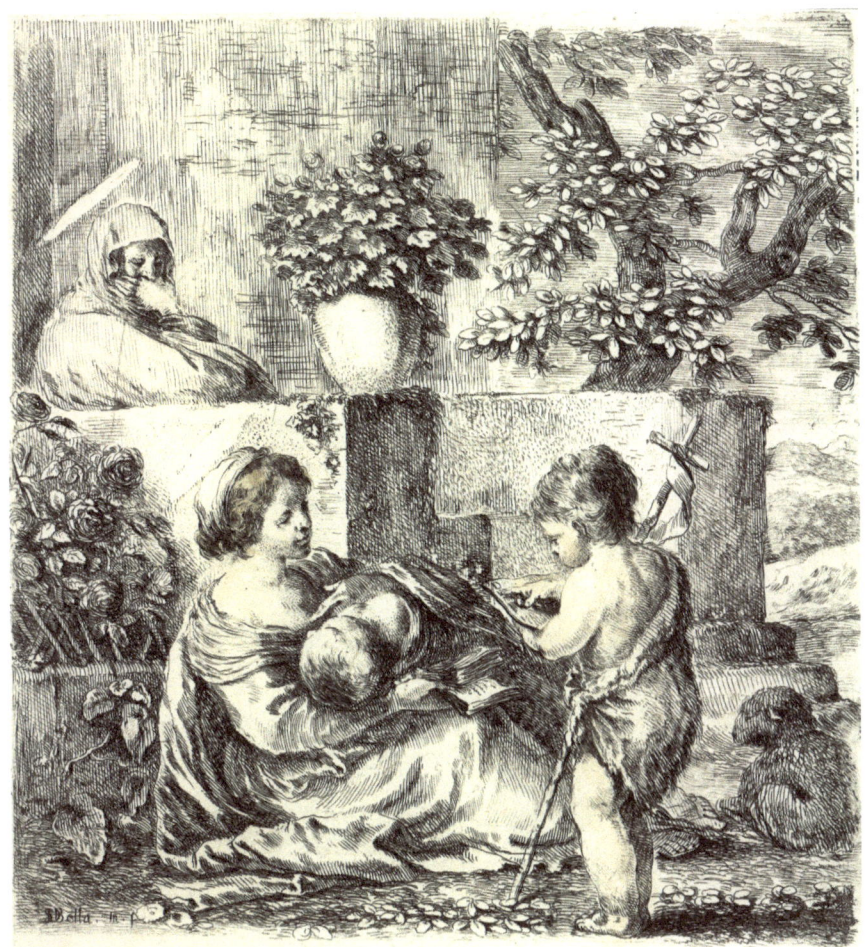

Cat. 24
Stefano della Bella (1610-1664), Italian
Virgin and Child with St. John, 1641
5 7/8" x 4 13/16"
Etching
73-G-445

In this garden setting, Mary cradles the swaddled sleeping Child as the young John the Baptist stands before them. Elizabeth, John's mother and Mary's cousin, protectively watches over the scene from behind a low wall. The elderly woman's attitude is one of melancholy, as she places hand to chin, contemplating what is to come.

Allusions to Christ's mission on earth abound in the print. The infant John is dressed in a hair shirt, which he will wear during his stay in the desert as an adult. He carries a staff in the shape of a cross. He also carries a book, and points to the word DEUS written it.[1] This refers to John's role in foretelling that Christ was the son of God, the Messiah. The recumbent lamb to his right is a symbol of the sacrifice that Christ will undertake as an adult.[2] The potted ivy on the low wall refers to His resurrection, because its leaves appear never to die but remain always green.[3] The tree in the right background, with its split branches, might refer to the wood of the cross of Christ's crucifixion. The rose behind Mary refers to her immaculate conception and to her role as the pure vessel for Christ's incarnation.[4] TC

1   Alessandro Baudi di Vesme and Phyllis Dearborn Massar, *Stefano della Bella, catalogue raisonné* (New York: Collectors Edition, 1971), vol. 1, 47 and vol. 2, 10 II/IV.

2   Geroge Ferguson, *Signs and Symbols in Christian Art* (New York: Oxford University Press, 1954), 33.

3   Ibid., 33.

4   Ibid., 37-38. Mary is often called the "rose without thorns."

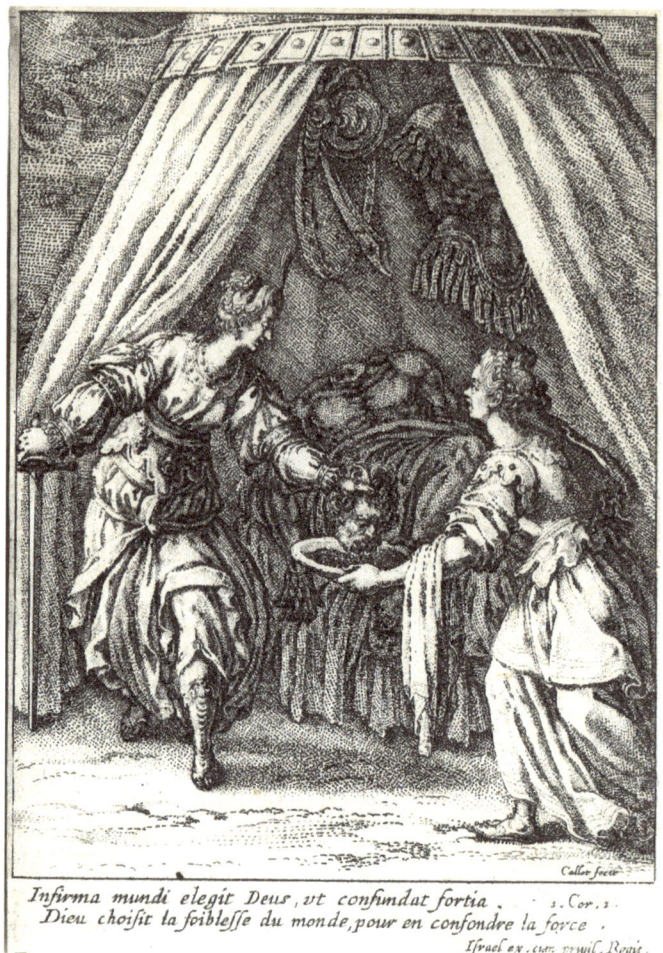

Infirma mundi elegit Deus, ut confundat fortia. 1.Cor.1
Dieu choisit la foiblesse du monde, pour en confondre la force.

Israel ex. cum privil. Regis.

Cat. 25
Jacques Callot (1592-1635), French
Judith with the Head of Holofernes, c. 1630
3 15/16" x 2 11/16"
Etching
76-B-1(g)5

The story of this small print is from the Old Testament's *Book of Judith*. Here the elegantly dressed Jewish princess Judith, sword in hand, places the newly severed head of the Assyrian general Holofernes on a charger proffered by her young handmaiden. By this act, Judith courageously freed the Jewish people from persecution.[1] The two women move vigorously in the space, while the general's decapitated body lays snugly in his tent canopy bed or pavillon, his armor hanging impotently from the ceiling. The story of Judith and Holofernes was a very popular subject in the Baroque period, although one rarely tackled by Callot.[2]

A great innovator in etching techniques, Callot used stippling, or a dotting of short lines, made entirely with the etching needle's point, to create shadow and texture. He abandoned stippling soon after this print in favor of other techniques.[3] SD

1   The inscription is from the New Testament's *First Letters to the Corinthians*. The passage translates as "God chose the weak to shame the strong." It provides commentary on the Old Testament story.

2   Helen Diane Russell and Jeffrey Blanchard, *Jacques Callot: Prints and Related Drawings* (Washington, DC: National Gallery of Art, 1975), 206; and Elena Ciletti, "Judith Imagery as Catholic Orthodoxy in Counter-Reformation Italy," in *The Sword of Judith: Judith Studies across the Disciplines*, eds. Kevin R. Brine, Elena Ciletti and Henrike Lähnemann (Cambridge: Open Book, 2010), 345-68.

3   Russell and Blanchard, *Jacques Callot*, 206.

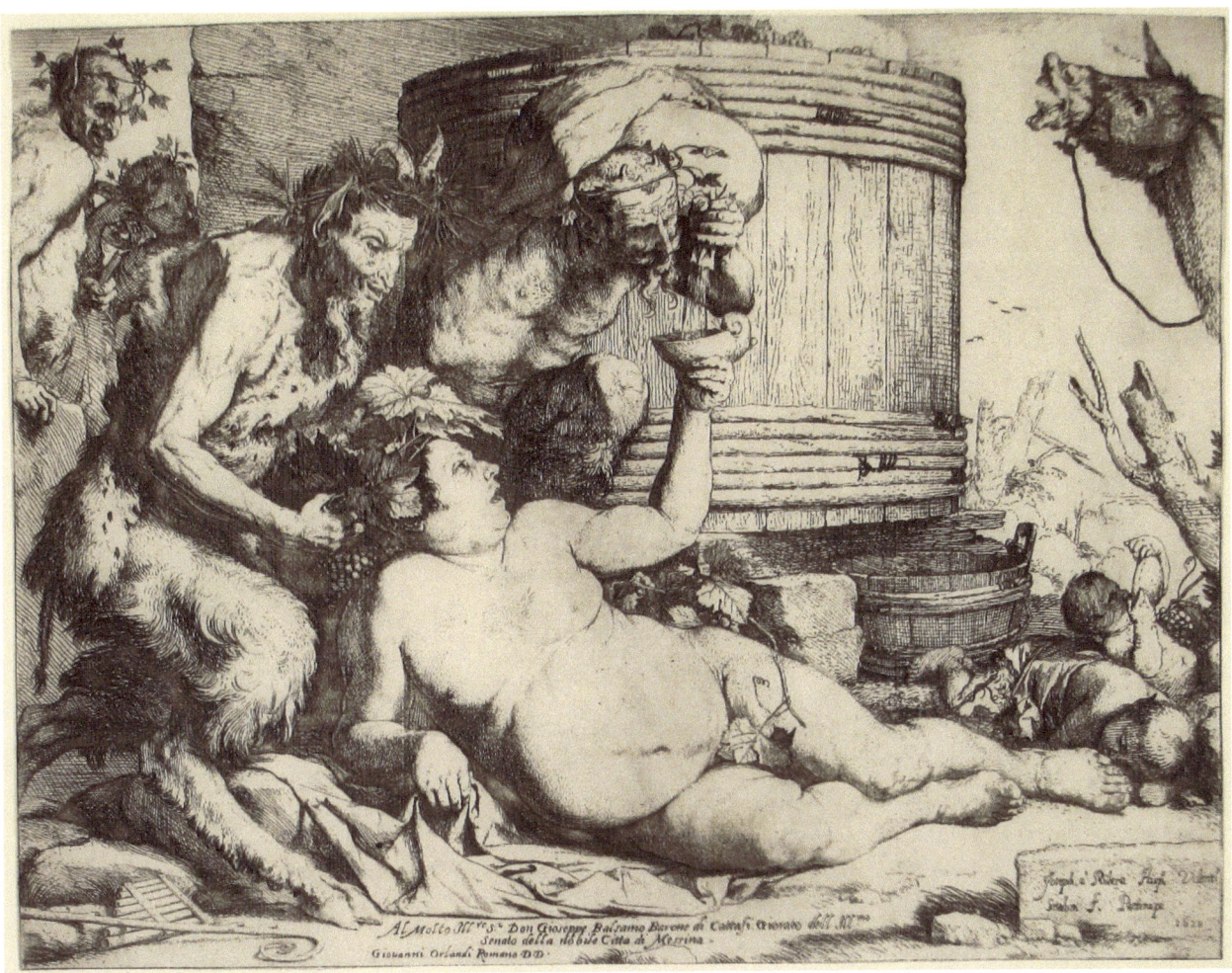

Cat. 26
Jusepe de Ribera (1591-1652), Spanish, active in Italy
The Drunken Silenus, 1628
10 $^{11}/_{16}$" x 14"
Etching and engraving
77-G-746

The painter Ribera was an occasional etcher. Most of his prints date from early in his career, in the 1620s. Arguably the most stunning one is that of Silenus, the perpetually drunken companion to Bacchus.[1] The image is a slight variation of his painting of the same subject commissioned by a Flemish merchant living in Naples. Both include the rotund reclining figure of Silenus, bedecked only in grape leaves, and attended by satyrs. Art historians believe this etched image is more powerful than the painting, despite its lack of color, because it gives greater emphasis to the irrational hedonism of the Bacchic delights. In this version, the satyrs appear more animal than human, Silenus' donkey seems to laugh in derision, and the wine-loving putti at his feet are beyond sentience.[2] Ribera's etching technique, which produces luscious textures throughout the print, aids in conveying the sensual decadence of the scene.[3] MD

1   Jonathan Brown, *Jusepe de Ribera: prints and drawings* (Princeton: Princeton University, 1973), 18-19, 75-76 and 107-108; and Marcus S. Sopher and Claudia Lazzaro, *Seventeenth-Century Prints* (Stanford: Stanford Art Gallery, 1978), 93-95.

2   Brown, *Jusepe de Ribera*, 26.

3   There are two inscriptions on the print. The one on the left identifies Ribera as a Neapolitan. The one on the base of the print was added by the publisher Giovanni Orlandi, who came to own the plate.

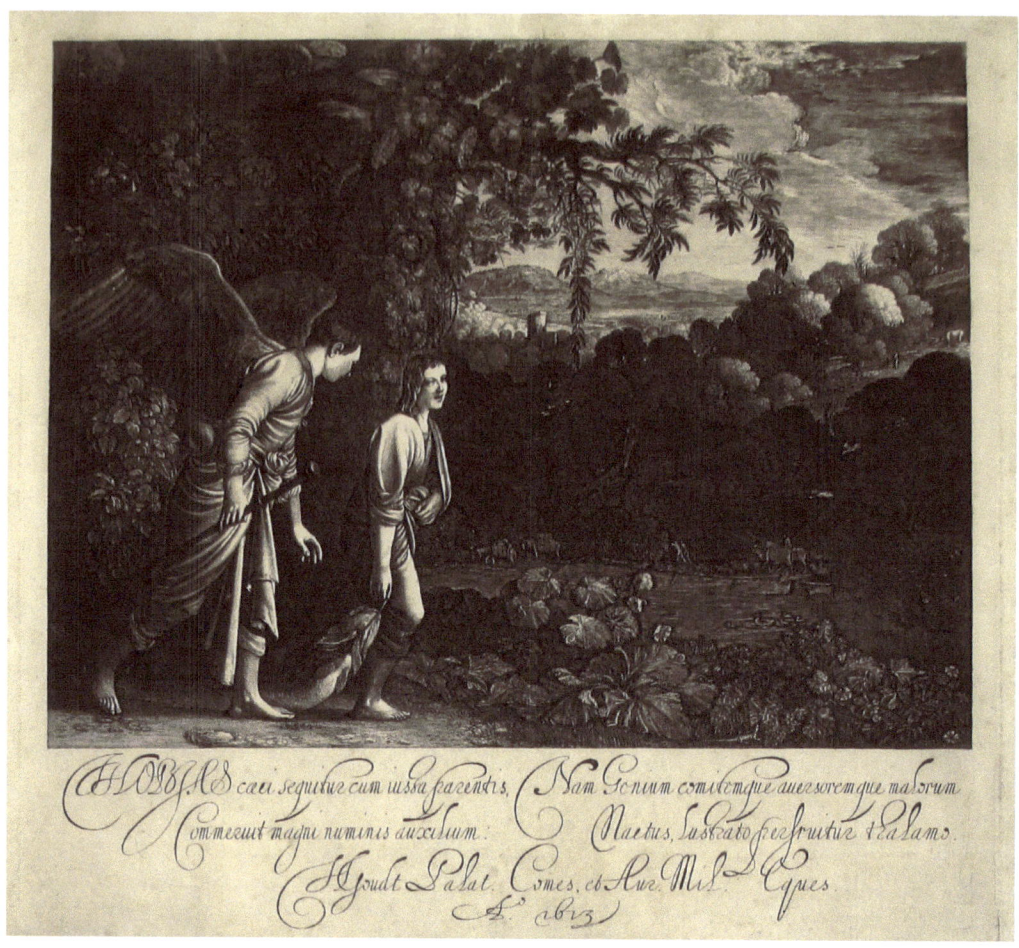

Cat. 27
Hendrick Goudt (1583-1648), Dutch
After Adam Elsheimer (1578-1610), German, active in Italy
Tobias and the Angel, 1613
10 1/8" x 10 9/16"
Engraving
77-G-776

Elsheimer's small oil paintings on copper, featuring landscapes with figures and magnificent light effects, were popular in Rome, where he made his career, and beyond. This print reproduces his lost painting of a scene from the *Book of Tobit* in the Old Testament.[1] With one arm, Tobit's young son Tobias drags the large fish he tackled at the angel Raphael's command, in order to extract medicinal oil to heal his father's blindness. Tobias' other arm is in a sling because of injuries he sustained in the battle with the fish. In the landscape are Oriental poppies and rhubarb, plants then exotic to Europe and well known for their medicinal properties.[2]

The relationship between the painter Elsheimer and the engraver Goudt was an unusual and strained one. Goudt was from a wealthy noble family, and yet he apprenticed as Elsheimer's student. He lent money to his financially-strapped master, and as part of the repayment Goudt came to own, reproduce, and earn revenue from some of Elsheimer's most valuable paintings.[3] AH

1   Keith Andrews, *Adam Elsheimer: Paintings, Drawings, Prints* (London: Phaidon, 1977), 154, notes that there are two painted copies, one in London, and another in Copenhagen.

2   Rüdiger Klessman, Emilie E.S. Gordenker and Christian Tico Seifert, *Adam Elsheimer 1578-1610* (Edinburgh: National Gallery of Scotland, 2006), 166-167, 188; and Andrews, *Adam Elsheimer*, 26.

3   Klessman, Gordenker and Seifert, *Adam Elsheimer*, 30-31. Goudt's signature at the base of the print is larger than was typical. It is as large as the inscription explaining the story.

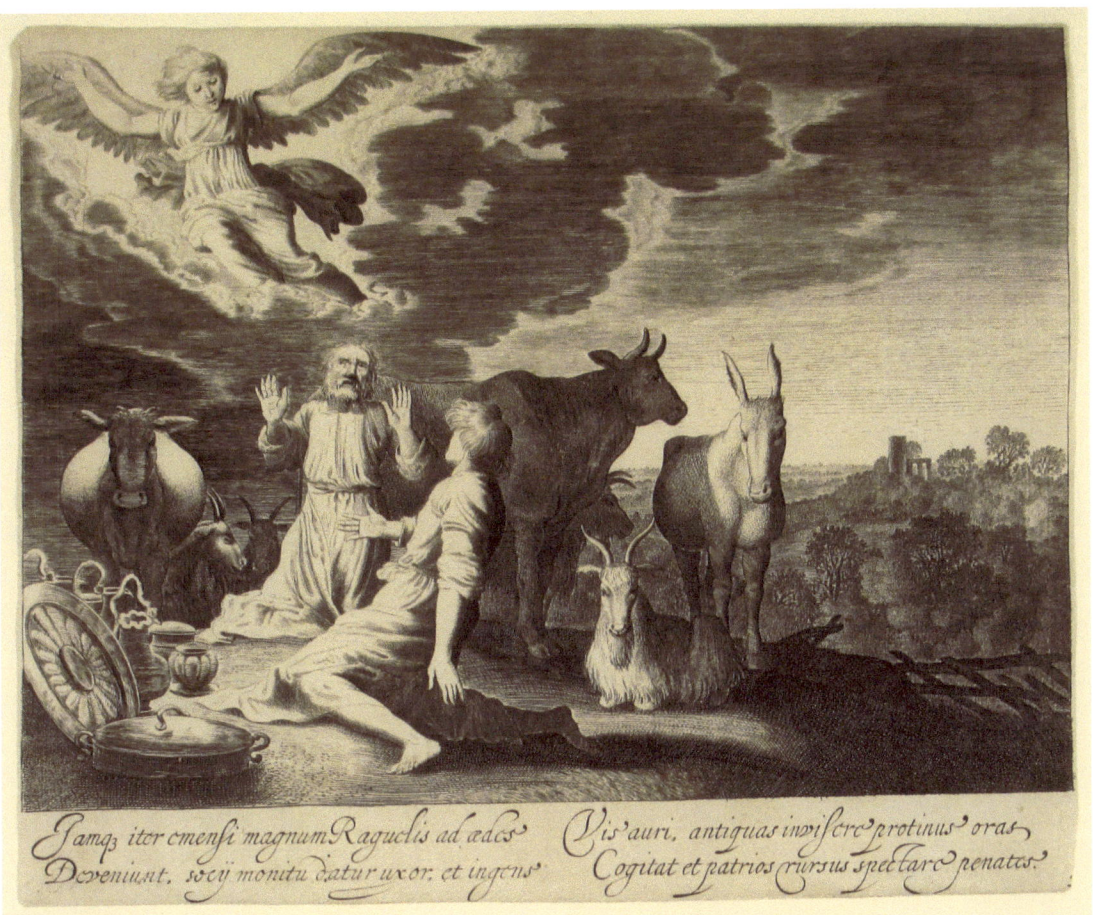

Jamq; iter emenfi magnum Raguelis ad ædes   Vis'auri, antiquas invifere protinus'oras
Deveniunt, socij monitu eatur uxor, et ingens   Cogitat et patrios riursus spectare penates.

Cat. 28
Jan van de Velde II (c. 1593-1641), Dutch
After Moses van Uyttenbroeck (1595-1647), Dutch
The Angel Departing from Tobit and Tobias
From the series *Story of Tobias and Angel*, c. 1630
5 3/16" x 6 1/4"
Etching and engraving
80-G-1079(4)

In this print of the final scene from the Book of Tobit, Tobias' blind father Tobit has regained his sight.[1] The angel Raphael had been instrumental in restoring the old man's health, and also the family's good fortune, by helping Tobias obtain a medicinal cure. However, Raphael did not reveal himself as an angel until all had been accomplished. The print captures the moment he reveals his true nature, as a light-filled creature, returning to the heavens. Below him, bathed in the divine light, kneel the startled father and son.[2]

A still life of a well-crafted metal serving dish and some ewers can be seen in the lower left. A donkey, cows and horned sheep, all oddly shadowed in the angel's glow, surround the father and son. They are indicators that 17th-century Dutch viewers would recognize as signs that the family's material wealth was restored. Historians have noted that the story of Tobit and Tobias was one that had resonance for the Dutch, accustomed to living with economic ups and downs.[3] AH

1   On the artists, see Clifford S. Ackley, ed., *Printmaking in the Age of Rembrandt* (Boston: Museum of Fine Arts, 1981), 70-72 and 195.

2   The inscription relates the story.

3   On the Dutch economy, see Jan De Vries, and Ad van der Woude, *The First Modern Economy: Success, Failure, and Perseverance of the Dutch Economy, 1500-1815* (Cambridge: Cambridge University Press, 1997). On the resonance of the story of Tobias, see Simon Schama, *Rembrandt's Eyes* (New York: Alfred A. Knopf, 1999), 238-41. Rembrandt depicted the story many times; see Julius Held, *Rembrandt and the Book of Tobit* (Northampton, MA: Gehenna Press, 1964).

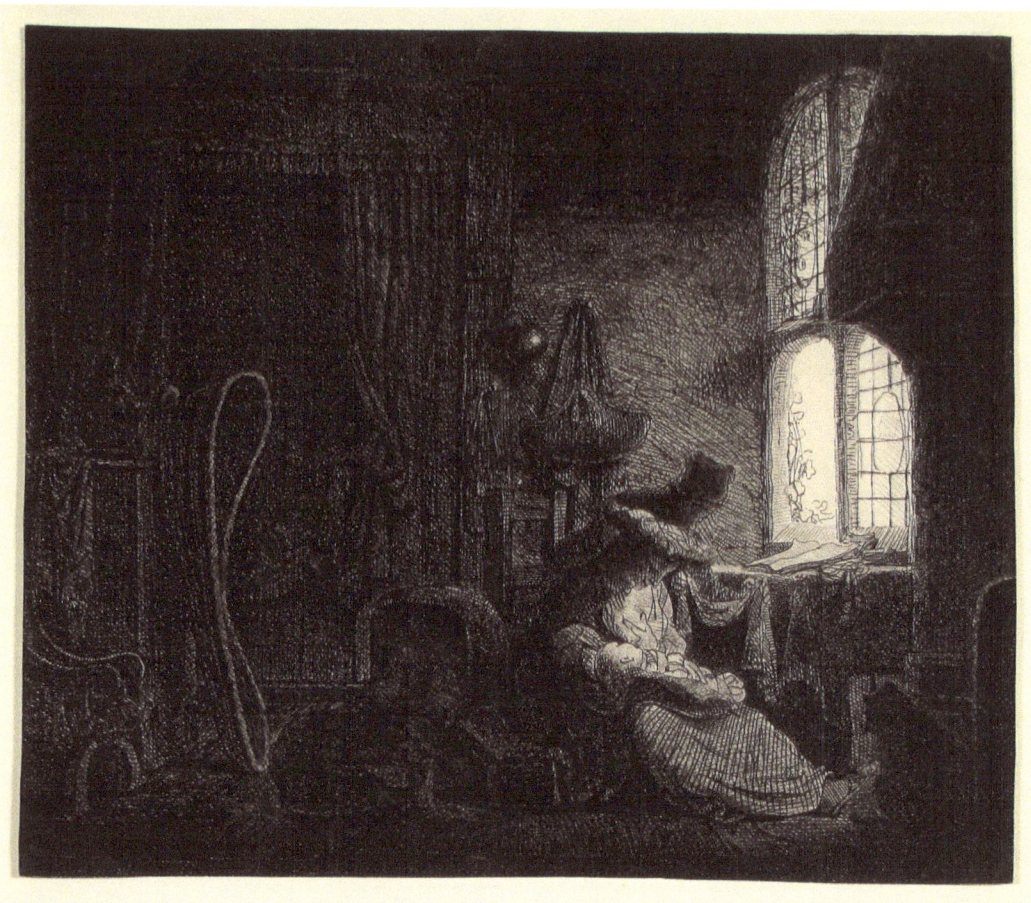

Cat. 29
Ferdinand Bol (1616-1680), Dutch
Holy Family in an Interior, 1643
7 1/8" x 8 3/8"
Etching, drypoint, and engraving
75-G-530

Bol's work exhibits the influence of Rembrandt, from whom Bol learned how to paint.[1] This *Holy Family in an Interior* is similar to some etchings and paintings by Rembrandt.[2] The attentive Joseph bends over the seated Mary, who suckles the baby. Both father and mother model behaviors expected of 17th-century Dutch families.[3] The family cat watches from the right foreground. They all occupy a Dutch domestic interior outfitted appropriately with a curtained bed, a cradle, and a table covered by a carpet. In front of the bed is a bakermat, a collapsible wicker seat for nursing mothers.[4]

The composition is like that of many Dutch 17th-century interiors, with a window at the far side, providing the only source of light in the darkened room. It creates dramatic and significant highlights on the family, and especially on the divine Child at Mary's breast, and obscures much of the setting in which Bol has placed the Holy Family. IM, ET

1   Albert Blankert, *Ferdinand Bol (1616-1680), Rembrandt's Pupil* (Doornspijk: Davaco, 1982), 15-25.

2   Michael Cole, ed., *The Early Modern Painter-Etcher* (University Park: The Pennsylvania State University Press, 2006), 133-134; Linda Stone-Ferrier, *Dutch Prints of Daily Life: Mirrors of Life or Masks of Morals?* (Lawrence, KS: University of Kansas Press, 1983), 68-69; and Clifford S. Ackley, ed., *Printmaking in the Age of Rembrandt* (Boston: Museum of Fine Arts, 1989), 155.

3   Laurinda Dixon, *Perilous Chastity: Women and Illness in Pre-Enlightenment Art and Medicine* (Ithaca: Cornell University Press, 1995), 159-167; and Mariët Westermann, *A Worldly Art: the Dutch Republic, 1585-1719* (New York: Harry N. Abrams, 1996), 119-129. See also Westermann, C. Willemijn Fock, Eric van Sluijer and H. Perry Chapman, *Art and Home: Dutch Interiors in the Age of Rembrandt* (Zwolle: Waanders, 2000).

4   Klaske Muizelaar and Derek Phillips, *Picturing Men and Women in the Dutch Golden Age: Paintings and People in Historical Perspective* (New Haven: Yale University Press, 2003), 42-61; and Peter Thornton, *Seventeenth-Century Interior Decoration in England, France and Holland* (New Haven: Yale University Press, 1979), 159, 207-208, 241-43.

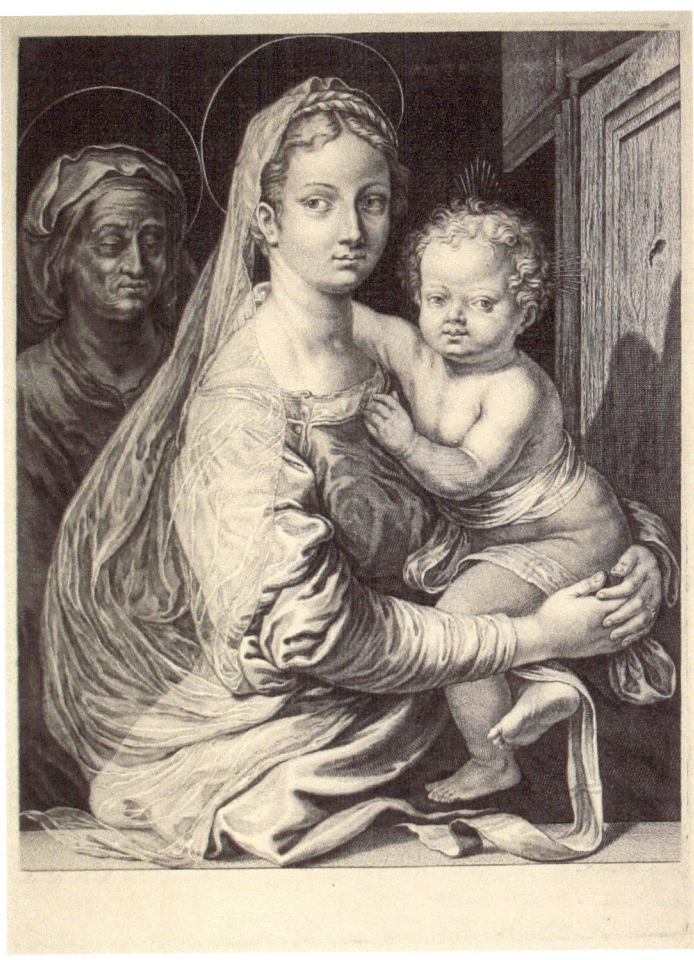

Cat. 30
Jeremias Falck (c. 1609/10-1677), Polish
After painting by School of Raphael (1483-1520), Italian
Virgin and Child with St. Anne, c. 1655-58
from *Cabinet Reynst, Variarum imaginum a celeberrimis
artificibus pictarum Caelaturae* (Amsterdam, 1660-1671)
15 3/4" x 11 9/16"
Engraving
02-G-3268

The art collection of the Reynst brothers was as famous as it was unusual in 17th-century Netherlands. The brothers were successful merchants and partners, with Gerard living in Amsterdam and Jan in Venice.[1] Together, from 1639 to 1668, they amassed a significant collection of paintings and antiquities in a "cabinet", i.e., in display rooms in Gerard's residence. The large number of paintings by Italian masters such as Titian and Tintoretto, as well as 17th-century painters such as Guido Reni and Guercino, distinguished the Reynst collection.[2] Typically Dutch collectors preferred paintings by Dutch artists.[3]

Gerard envisioned a publication of prints of some of the major works in the collection. After his death in 1658, the project was continued by his brother Jan, and then by his widow; it was eventually published as *Variarum imaginum*. Jeremias Falck created 12 of the 34 prints in the publication. He was a fine reproductive engraver who arrived in Amsterdam from Gdansk around 1655 to work for Gerard. Falck believed himself to be extremely lucky because he was well compensated for his labors.[4] He is lauded for capturing the subtle shading found in the original paintings.

The painting of *The Virgin and Child with St. Anne* was lost after the collection was dispersed.[5] SD

1   Anne-Marie Logan, *The 'Cabinet' of the Brothers Gerard and Jan Reynst* (Amsterdam: North-Holland Publishing Company, 1979), 19-35.

2   Ibid., 37-65.

3   Ibid., 100-101. There were about 200 Italian paintings in the collection. Logan states that, outside of Italy, only the Count of Arundel's collection surpassed that of the Reynst brothers. Similarly, antiquities were not often collected in the Netherlands, but the Reynst had over 100 works.

4   Ibid., 40, 43-44. Cornelis Visscher (1629-1658, Dutch) produced another 12 of the engravings; the rest were assigned to various printmakers.

5   Part of the Cabinet Reynst was sold to the Dutch Republic and thereafter offered to Charles II as part of diplomatic efforts with England. The offer was called "the Dutch Gift." See Ibid., 75-86. There is no consensus on the attribution of the *Virgin and Child with Saint Anne*. Some believe the original painting to be by Raphael; others, by Andrea del Sarto or Perino del Vago. See Ibid., 138.

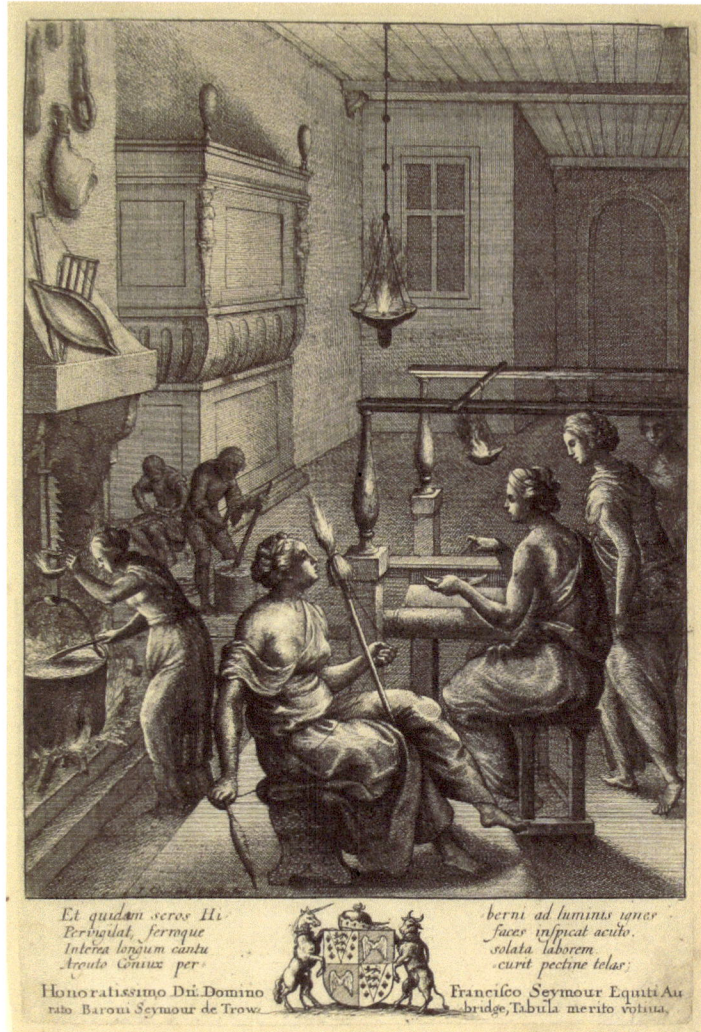

Et quidam seros Hi-
Pervigilat, ferroque
Interea longum cantu
Arouto Coniux per-

berni ad luminis igner
faces inspicat acuto.
solata laborem
curit pectine telas;

Honoratissimo Dñi Domino
rato Baroni Seymour de Trow-

Francisco Seymour Equiti Au-
bridge, Tabula merito votiua.

Cat. 31
Wenceslaus Hollar (1607-1677), Bohemian
After a drawing by Francis Cleyn (c. 1582-1658),
German
Women at Work
From John Ogilby, *The works of Publius Virgilius Maro*
(London: Thomas Warren, c. 1654)
11 $\frac{11}{16}$" x 7 $\frac{7}{8}$"
Etching and drypoint
13-G-3552
Gift of Dr. Klare Scarborough

Hollar created this print to illustrate John Ogilby's translation of stories from the Roman poet Virgil. Ogilby was
a dedicated translator of classic texts. He created illustrated publications of these texts as a means to educate
children. Hollar, along with other printmakers, worked
for him, cutting the designs created by Francis Cleyn.[1]

In this scene from the story of Ulysses, his wife Penelope
weaves cloth with the help of her three female servants.
By working diligently, she wards off suitors who believe
that she is a beautiful widow. However, Ulysses is not
dead. He is having unexpected adventures on his long
return voyage home from the Trojan War. Thus, Penelope represents the faithful and industrious wife. She
served as a good example for 17th-century English society, whose women often kept the household running
while their merchant husbands were away at sea.[2]

The scene of the ancient story is placed inside another
scene, a 17th-century interior in which servants perform
common household tasks. One female servant stirs a
large cauldron on the hearth while two boys whittle
stakes in the background.[3] Light sources strike the two
scenes differently. The hearth fire illuminates the 17th-
century servant, while the oil lamps cast dramatic highlights and shadows on Penelope and her helpers. SD

1   Richard Pennington, *A Descriptive Catalogue of the Etched Work of Wencelaus
    Hollar 1607-1677* (Cambridge: Cambridge University Press, 1982), 39-40, 42. This
    print is from a revised edition of *The Works of Publius Virgilius Maro*, translated by
    John Ogilby and printed by Thomas Warren. On their use to educate children, see
    Katherine S. Van Eerde, *Wencelaus Hollar: Delineator of his Times* (Charlottesville:
    University of Virginia Press, 1970), 47.

2   Laurinda Dixon, *Perilous Chastity: Women and Illness in Pre-Enlightenment Art and
    Medicine* (Ithaca: Cornell University Press, 1995),131-138.

3   For discussion of the image-within-an-image motif, common to Dutch and Spanish
    Baroque art, see John F. Moffitt, Sheldon Richmond and David Carrier, "On Pictures
    Within Pictures,"*Leonardo* 12, no. 4 (Autumn, 1979): 350-51.

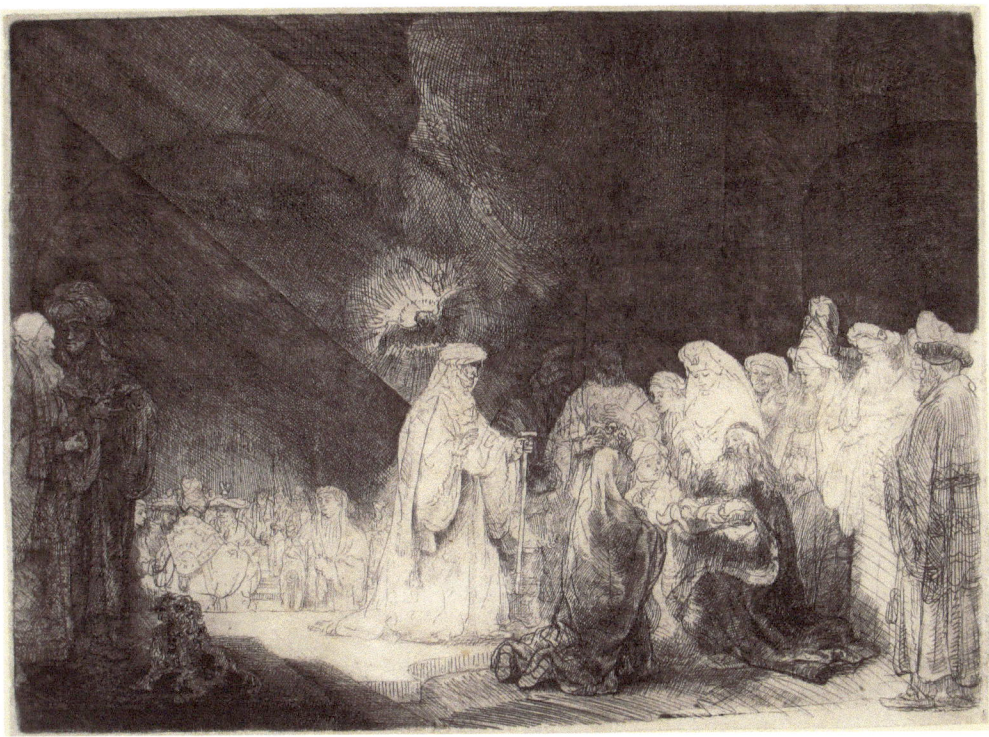

Cat. 32
Rembrandt van Rijn (1606-1669), Dutch
Presentation in the Temple, c. 1640
11 ½" x 8 ½"
Etching and drypoint
72-G-352

Luke 2: 22-39 narrates the story of Mary and Joseph presenting the Christ Child in the Temple of Jerusalem. This Jewish religious practice required parents to bring a child to the Temple forty days after its birth. Mary and Joseph bring Jesus to the Temple and encounter two individuals often called the last Old Testament prophets. One is the elderly scholar Simeon, who received God's promise that he would not die until he had met the Messiah. The other is an elderly widow Anna, known as the Prophetess, who recognized the Child as the Messiah.

Rembrandt's composition highlights the two prophets in this version of the narrative. In the cavernous architectural setting of the Temple, the aged Simeon kneels and holds the Child. He declares to the solemn Mary that she and the Child will know undergo great tribulations in their lives, as the gathered faithful look concerned. The tall Anna, wearing the Judaic prayer shawl, strides towards the group, her hands extended as she recognizes the Messiah. The light emanating from the Holy Spirit, positioned above Anna's head, spotlights the Child. In the left foreground of the print, untouched by the light, are a Saducee and a Pharisee, deep in argument, and curiously, a dog.[1]

Rembrandt was a careful reader of the Bible and other religious texts, as his images attest. Like many 17th-century Dutch Christians at the time, he had a special interest in typology, which was the practice of reading the Old Testament as prophesy and the New Testament as fulfillment of that prophesy.[2] The *Presentation in the Temple*, however, illustrates the collision of the Old and New Testament narratives, in which the characters of the first recognize their prophetic work as completed. Rembrandt's print illustrates the significance of this moment. KS

1   Christopher White and Karel G. Boon. *Rembrandt's Etchings: an illustrated critical catalogue* (Amsterdam: Van Gendt & Co., 1969), vol. 1, 25, vol. 2, 38 (B49/II); and Shelly Perlove and Larry Silver, *Rembrandt's Faith: Church and Temple in the Dutch Golden Age* (University Park: Pennsylvania State University Press, 2009), 162-217, esp. 202-17.

2   Perlove and Silver, *Rembrandt's Faith*, 59.

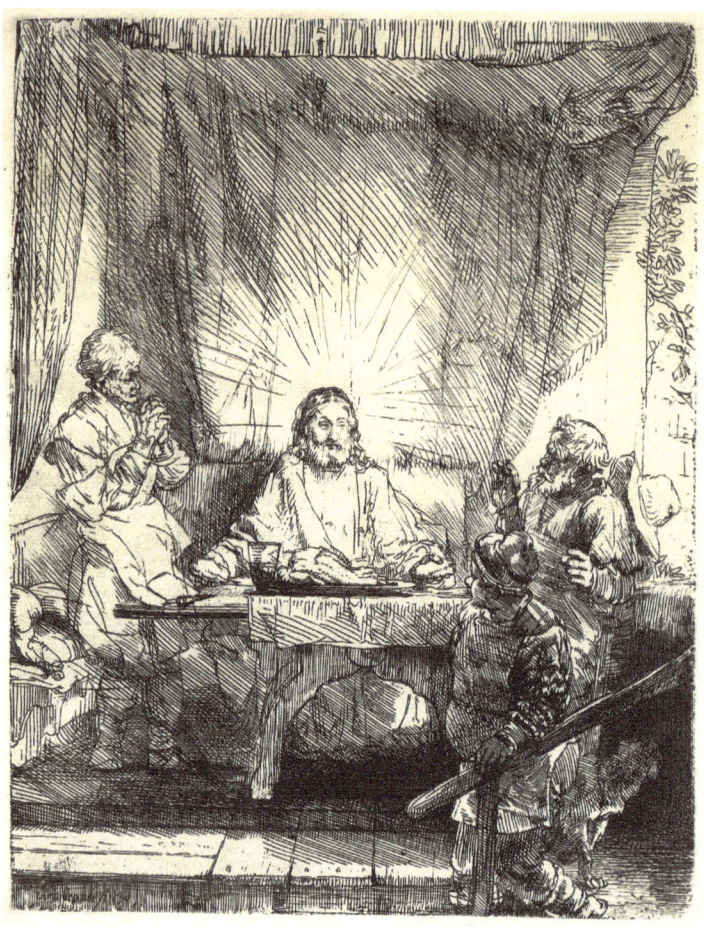

Cat. 33
Rembrandt van Rijn (1606-1669), Dutch
Supper at Emmaus (larger plate), 1654
6 1/2" x 5"
Etching
82-G-1222
Gift of Dr. and Mrs. William K. Sherwin

Rembrandt depicts the resurrected Christ at the table after breaking bread. His two companions have heretofore not recognized Him. One suddenly figures it out and reacts by getting on his feet, hands together in prayer. The other, who is the object of Christ's direct gaze, is just beginning to understand. This man falls back, his hat falling from his head. A third character, probably the innkeeper's son, walks down a staircase in the foreground. He is curious about what is happening but essentially remains unaware of the revelation.[1]

The light, emanating from the body of Christ, and particularly from his halo, falls on the figures in meaningful ways. The man in prayer is almost fully in light, while the boy is nearly fully in shadow. Light and shadow dapple the startled man.

Rembrandt revisited this subject of the *Supper at Emmaus* a number of times, as he often did with other biblical stories. He sometimes responded to other artist's versions of the stories and sometimes to his own. This habit allowed him to explore fresh insights into the biblical stories.[2] OA, SD

1   Christopher White and Karel G. Boon, *Rembrandt's Etchings: an illustrated critical catalogue* (Amsterdam: Van Gendt & Co., 1969), vol. 1, 48-49 and vol. 2, 84, B87/I. For the biblical passage, see *Luke* 24: 13-32.

2   Erik Hinterding, Ger Luijten and Martin Royalton-Kisch, *Rembrandt the Printmaker* (Chicago and London: Fitzroy Dearborn Publishers, 2000), 18-21.

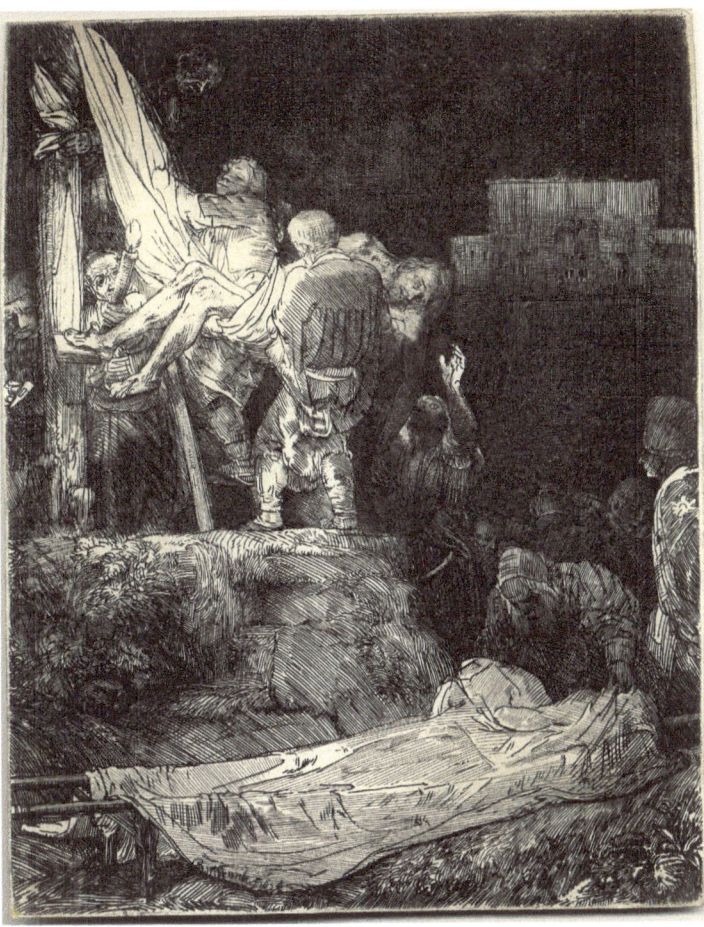

Cat. 34
Rembrandt van Rijn (1606-1669), Dutch
Descent from the Cross by Torchlight, 1654
5" x 6 ¹/₂"
Etching
76-G-587

In most versions of the *Descent from the Cross*, the body of Christ is upright, having just been separated from the cross. In this harrowing image, He is horizontal and the Cross is barely visible. The focus is shifted to the men doing the tough but necessary work of deposing and burying the body. A man with his back to the viewer supports the body, while another struggles to disentangle the white cloth cradling it. Still another begins to remove the last nail from the foot of Christ, still pinioning Him to the cross. Below, Joseph of Arimathea prepares the awaiting shroud. The light emitted from a torch held by one of the men highlights these actions. From the shadows, the grieving Mary reaches up towards her son.[1]

By 1654, Rembrandt was commanding high prices for his etchings. He created original compositions, rather than copies of his paintings. In addition, he made efforts to make prints somewhat "uncommon" or distinct in order to enhance their desirability to collectors. For example, he dramatically altered his plates by reworking them, by inking them in different ways, and by printing on different types of papers.[2] In this case, he created only one state of the print, thus ensuring limited copies and the print's value to collectors.[3] SD

1   Erik Hinterding, Ger Luijten Luijten and Martin Royalton-Kisch, *Rembrandt the Printmaker* (Chicago and London: Fitzroy Dearborn Publishers, 2000), 306-308; and Christopher White and Karel G. Boon, *Rembrandt's Etchings: an illustrated critical catalogue* (Amsterdam: Van Gendt & Co., 1969), vol. 1, 46 and vol. 2, 80, B83.

2   Hinterding, Luijten and Royalton-Kisch, *Rembrandt the Printmaker*, 14-21. The term "uncommon" is Rembrandt's.

3   Ibid., 306. The early impressions are on Japanese paper; this impression is on laid paper. The plate is now in the Pierpont Morgan Library in New York City.

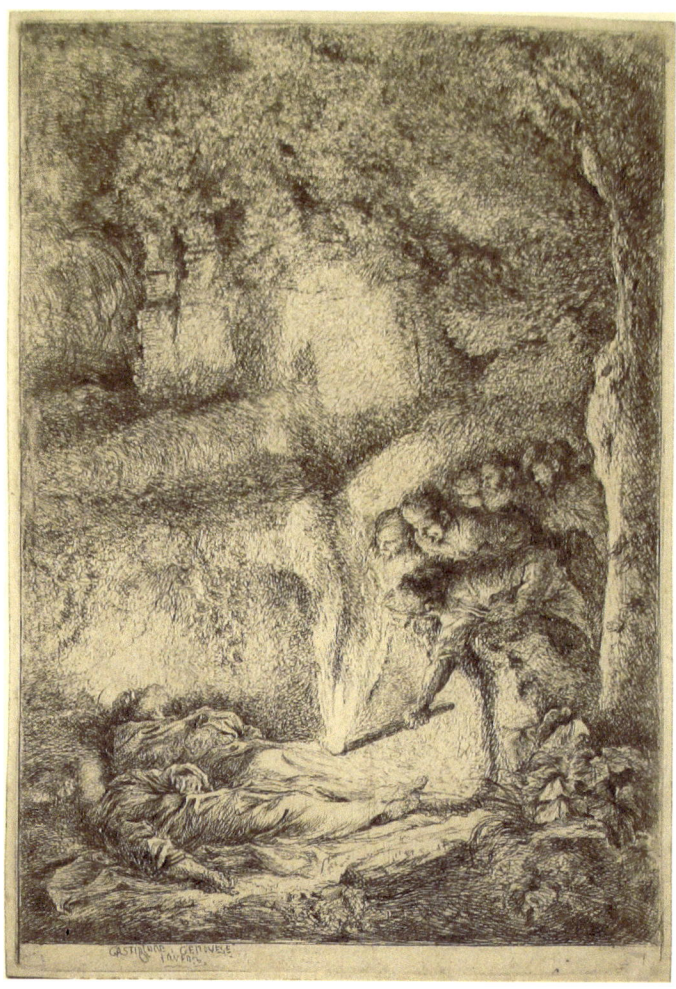

Cat. 35
Giovanni Benedetto Castiglione (c. 1609-1664), Italian
Finding of the Bodies of Sts. Peter and Paul, 1647-50
11 13/16" x 8 1/16"
Etching
81-G-1173

Castiglione's print of the discovery of the incorrupt bodies of the two pillar saints of the Catholic Church was based on an early Christian fresco.[1] Although apocryphal, it was a popular subject in 17th-century Catholic countries in the post-Reformation age. It reflected a desire to embrace Paul, who had been appropriated by the Protestants, as Peter's partner in founding the Church.

Castiglione depicts the dank recesses of the ancient catacombs outside Rome. An intense group of the faithful lean forward, and one figure extends a torch towards the discovery. In the foreground are the two prostate bodies of the saints, that of the elderly bearded Peter clutching his key, and that of the decapitated Paul perhaps gesturing the sign of the Holy Trinity.[2] The light bathes their bodies and then reflects upward, creating a wondrous atmosphere for the miraculous event.[3] SD

1   Anne Percy, *Giovanni Battista Castiglione: Master Draughtsman of the Italian Baroque* (Philadelphia: Philadelphia Museum of Art, 1970), 144-145, believes it derives from a fresco that once decorated the portico of Old St. Peter's. It was destroyed in 1609-10 to make room for the Baroque cathedral we see today, but is known from an engraving in Antonio Bosio, *Roma Sotterraneo* (Rome: Guglielmo Facciotti, 1632), 183. See also Paolo Bellini, *L'opera incise di Giovanni Benedetto Castligione* (Milan: Ripartizione cultura e spettacolo, 1982), 57.

2   In 1599, the incorrupt body of the decapitated Cecilia, a saint martyred around 230 C.E., was found in the catacombs. Legend has it that she took quite a long time to bleed to death after her neck was severed. In her suffering, she demonstrated her devotion to the faith by extending three fingers in a gesture indicating the Holy Trinity. The Roman Baroque sculptor Stefano Maderno captured the gesture in his sculpture, created in 1599-1600, now in the church of Santa Cecilia, Rome.

3   For Castiglione's technical achievements, see essay by Rachel Christie in this catalogue.

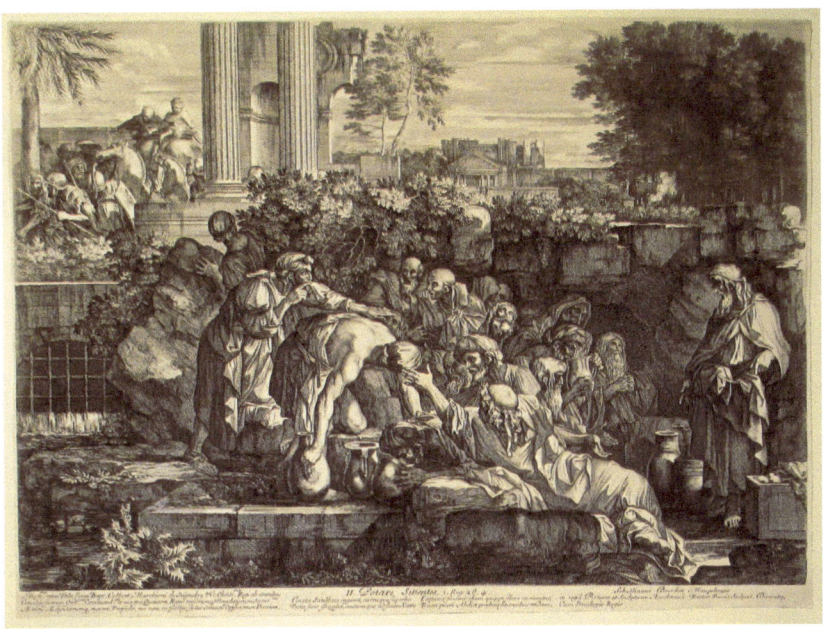

Cat. 36
Sébastien Bourdon (1616-1671), French
Giving Water to the Thirsty
From the series *The Seven Acts of Corporal Mercy*, 1666-71
17 1/8" x 23"
Engraving
74-G-500

The Christian concept of the Seven Acts of Corporal Mercy derives from Christ's words in *Matthew* 26: 35-36. The Acts include Feeding the Hungry, Giving Water to the Thirsty, Welcoming Strangers, Clothing the Naked, Comforting the Sick, Liberating Prisoners, and Burying the Dead.[1]

A talented painter as well as printmaker, Bourdon created seven paintings of the *Acts of Corporal Mercy* in 1666-68.[2] They were intended as a counterpart to the great classical Baroque artist Nicolas Poussin's *Sacrament* series of the 1640s, then owned by Jean-Baptiste Colbert, the Minister of Finance (and unofficially the Minister of Culture), for the newly empowered King Louis XIV.[3] Bourdon reproduced his own paintings in this series of engraved prints. In homage to Poussin, Bourdon carefully composed the scene, with staged figures against a studied background of classical buildings. At times he employed a method of creating highlights and shadows that recalls the dramatic Baroque art of Caravaggio's paintings, which he saw when he studied in Rome from 1636 to 1638. One can see this best in the bent figures on the left of the composition.

Bourdon chose an obscure Old Testament story (1 *Kings* 18: 4) to illustrate the merciful giving of water to those who are thirsty. The prophet Abias (or Obadiah) brought pitchers of water to the elderly prophets to escape persecution by the impious and depraved Queen Jezabel. Abias is the standing figure at the right. Some of the men drink as they cower behind a ruined stone wall, at whose base can be seen the grilled arched entry to an ancient water emissary. In the far left background, Jezabel can be seen leading a frenzied search for the prophets. The verse at the bottom of the print describes the scene. SD

1 Geraldine E. Fowle, "Sébastien Bourdon's *Acts of Mercy*: Their Significance as a Series," in *Hortus Imaginum: Essays in Western Art*, eds. Robert Enggass and Marilyn Stokstad (Lawrence: University of Kansas, 1975), 148.

2 Fowle, "Bourdon's *Acts of Mercy*," 147. The paintings are currently at the Ringling Museum in Sarasota, Florida. All but two are in bad condition and deemed beyond restoration efforts. See Jacques Thuillier, *Sébastien Bourdon, 1616-1671: catalogue critique et chronologique de l'oeuvre complet* (Paris: Réunion des musées nationaux, 2000), 411-17.

3 This is Nicolas Poussin's second set of Seven Sacrament paintings, painted in the 1640s for Paul Fréart, Sieur de Chantelou.

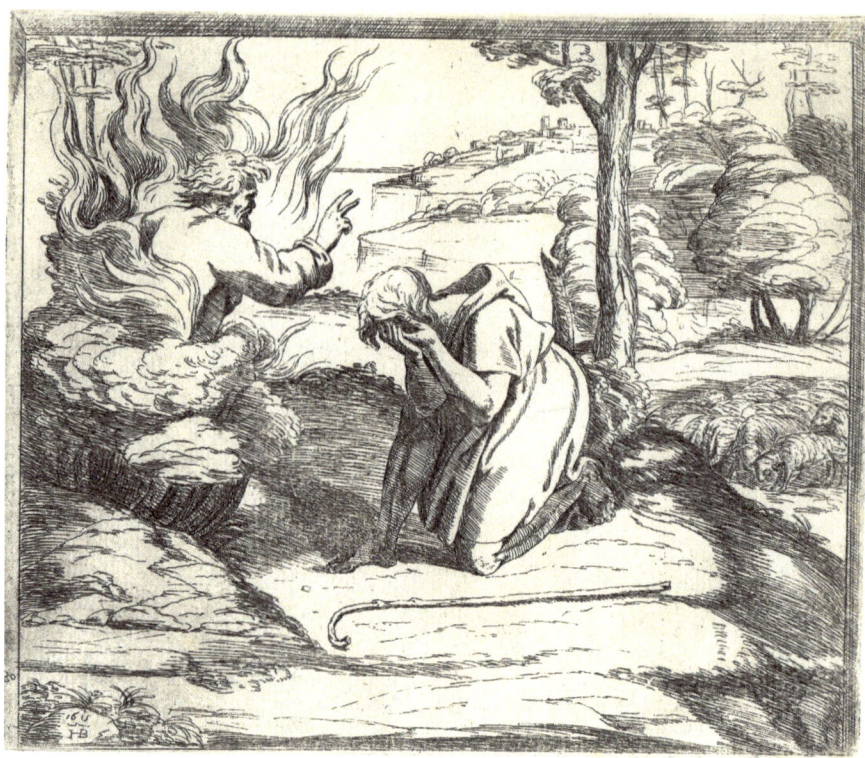

Cat. 37
Orazio Borgianni (c. 1578-1616) Italian
After fresco by Raphael (1483-1520), Italian
Moses and the Burning Bush, 1615
Etching
6 1/4" x 7 3/16"
Gift of Dr. Justin Tanis and James T. Tanis
13-G-3587

Today little studied, Raphael's frescoed cycle in the Loggia of Pope Leo X in the Vatican Palace, 1518-1519, was one of the most reproduced works of art in the 16th and 17th centuries. Four scenes from the Old Testament adorn the vault of each of the 13 bays of the loggia. They depict scenes from the Creation of the World to the Consecration of the Temple of Solomon.[1] This print illustrates a scene derived from *Exodus* 3:1-20. Moses has fallen to his knees before the flaming bush that would not burn. From the bush comes a voice. God commands him to lead the Israelites out of captivity in Egypt. The barefooted Moses covers his eyes in fear.[2]

Orazio Borgianni was one of many 17th-century artists to reproduce Raphael's frescos. Unbound and without a frontispiece, his prints of all 52 scenes were issued out of the well-known and successful publishing establishment of Giovanni Giacomo Rossi in Rome in 1615. The artist's monogram HB, for "Horatio" (a Latinized version of Orazio) Borgianni, appears on all the numbered prints.[3]

Borgianni is well known as a painter who adopted the style of Caravaggio in 1604 after he settled in Rome.[4] He turned to etching only in the last years of his short life. The loose and scratchy handling of the etchings, which privileges the poché line over cross-hatching, is characteristic of all Borgianni's graphic work.[5] TS

1   See Guida d'Italia del Touring Club Italiano, *Roma e Dintorni* (Milan: Settima Edizione, 1977), 579-80, for a list of the scenes. The 13th bay is decorated with major scenes from the Life of Christ.

2   Massimo Mussini, *La Bibbia di Raffaello: Scienza e scrittura nella stampa di riproduzione dei secoli XVI e XVII* (Brescia: Paideia, 1979), 58-79.

3   Ibid., 62, n. 2. Also see Alfredo Petrucci, *Il Caravaggio acquafortista e il mondo calcografico romano: L'Indovina, Leoni, Borgianni, Maggi, Villamena, Onofri, Mercati, Amici di Caravaggio* (Rome: Fratelli Palombi, 1956), 47-52.

4   Gianni Papi, *Orazio Borgianni* (Soncino: Edizioni dei Soncino, 1993), 7-19.

5   Ibid., 140-150, 199-201.

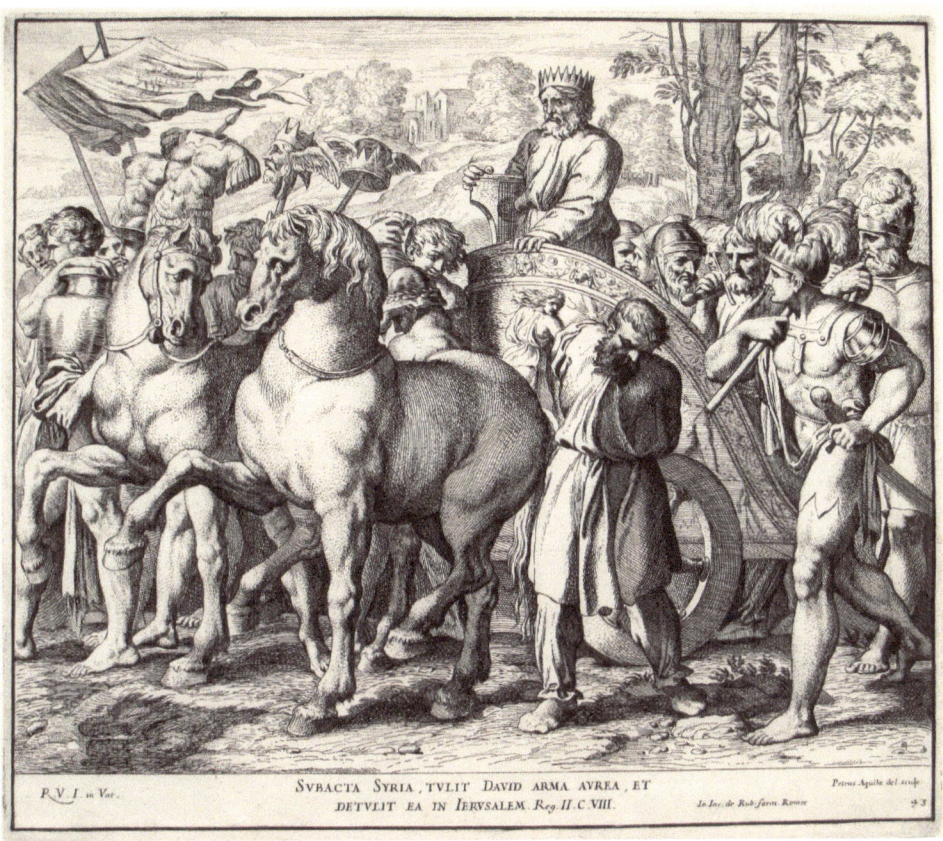

Cat. 38
Pietro Aquila (1619-1692), Italian
After fresco by Raphael (1483-1520), Italian
The Triumph of King David, 1674
From *Imagines Veteris ac Novi Testamenti a Raphaele Sanctio Urbinate in Vaticani Palatii* (Rome:
Giovanni Giacomo de' Rossi, 1674)
10" x 11 ³/₈"
Etching
81-G-1167

Prints of all 52 of Raphael's frescoed images of the Old Testament from the Loggia of Pope Leo X were assembled, bound and issued in *Imagines Veteris ac Novi Testamenti a Raphaele Sanctio Urbinate in Vaticani Palatii* in 1674. The publication was dedicated to Christina of Sweden, the exiled monarch who abdicated her throne after she embraced Catholicism. She settled in Rome and surrounded herself with artists, scholars, poets, and men of culture.[1]

Aquila was given the commission for some of the prints in the publication, including the frontispiece.[2] His etched interpretations of Raphael's frescoes stressed the pure forms, the logical shadowing and the appropriate expression in the master's composition. Raphael's style was studied and appreciated in late 17th-century Rome for its idealism. Pietro Bellori, an art critic and theorist at the court of Christina of Sweden, called for an idealism in the visual arts, advocating a classical Baroque style as opposed to the dramatic Baroque styles of Caravaggio and Bernini.[3] TS, SD

1   Massimo Mussini, *La Bibbia di Raffaello: Scienza e scrittura nella stampa di riproduzione dei secoli XVI e XVII* (Brescia: Paideia, 1979), 75-79.

2   Ibid., 77. Although also a painter, Aquila is known more for his 300 etchings. See Marcus S. Sopher and Claudia Lazzaro, *Seventeenth-Century Italian Prints* (Stanford: Stanford Art Gallery, 1978), 26.

3   Erwin Panofsky, *Idea: A Concept in Art Theory*, trans. Joseph Peake (Columbia: University of South Carolina Press, 1968), 103-11; and Tomaso Montanari, "Bellori and Christina of Sweden," in *Art History in the Age of Bellori: Scholarship and Cultural Politics in Seventeenth-Century Rome*, eds. Janis Bell and Thomas Willette (Cambridge: Cambridge University Press, 2002), 94-126. For more on Aquila and his reproductive prints, see Taylor Strickland's essay in this catalogue.

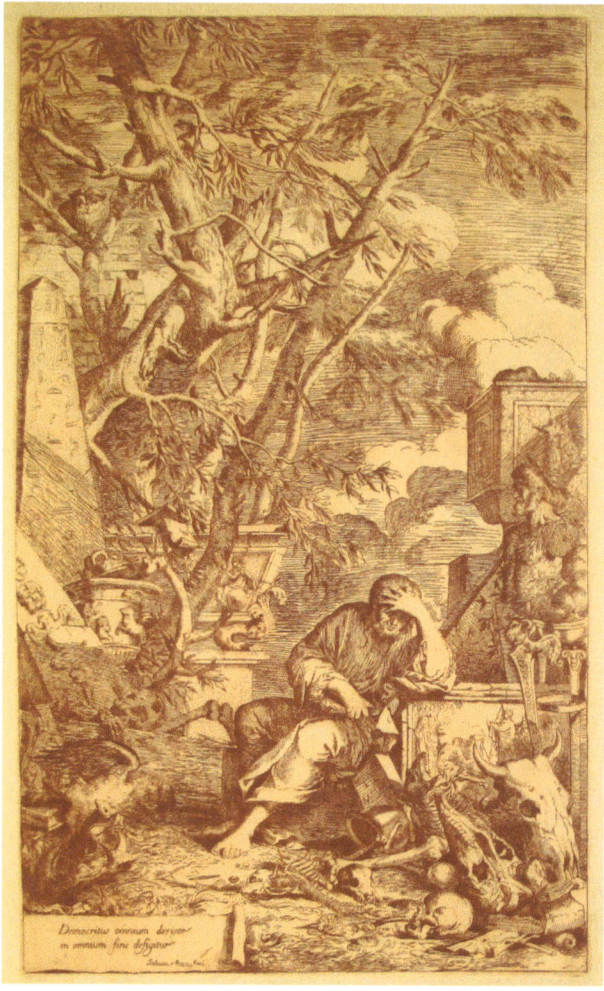

Cat. 39
Salvator Rosa (1615-1673), Italian
Democritus in Meditation, 1662
14 ¹/₂" x 8 ¹/₂"
Etching and drypoint
68-G-239

Democritus was known as the Laughing Philosopher because he mocked his fellow ancient Greeks for their follies. He was critical of their irrational reliance on material goods. The 17th-century artist Rosa sympathized with Democritus' beliefs. His depiction of the philosopher is unusual, however. Rosa illustrates Democritus as distraught. Democritus sits head in hand, in a melancholic attitude. It is difficult to see if he is laughing or crying. He is surrounded by many objects that suggest death and decay. The inscription informs us: "Democritus the mocker of all things is here stopped by the ending of all things." A pile of bones and skulls sit atop books and paint brushes, objects dear to Rosa. A broken obelisk and a ruined sarcophagus are nearby. More mysterious are the owls, which signify wisdom. There are two: one perched in the treetops and another dead on the ground.[1]

In this print, Rosa reproduced one of his most famous paintings, now in the Statens Museum in Copenhagen. The symbolic objects are more readable in the print than in the painting, but the print does not convey the somber tone of the original painting.[2] HM, AM

1   Richard Wallace, *The Etchings of Salvator Rosa* (Princeton: Princeton University Press, 1979), 261-66.

2   Jonathan Scott, *Salvator Rosa: His Life and Times* (New Haven and London: Yale University Press, 1995), 149-153. Rosa also changed some of the objects.

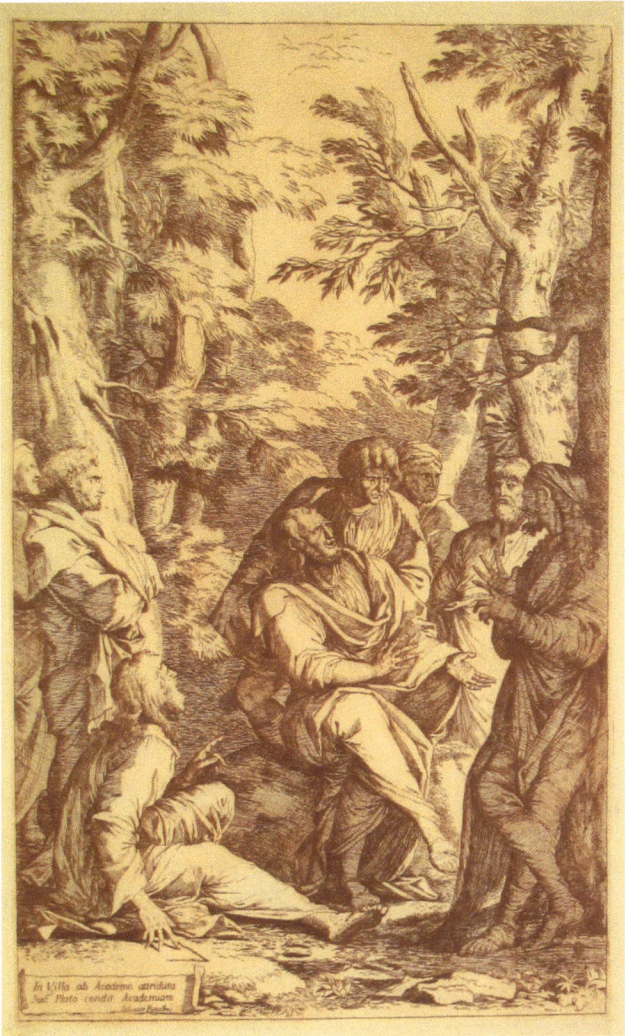

Cat. 40
Salvator Rosa (1615-1673), Italian
The Academy of Plato, c. 1662
18" x 10 7/8"
Etching and drypoint
68-G-238

In Rome in the 1660s, Rosa turned to printmaking as a means of establishing some financial independence from the patronage system in Italy. Printmaking allowed him to sell to international markets and to create his own subject matter. He chose subjects that reflected his great love of poetry and his passionate desire for learning.[1]

Plato's Academy is represented as a group of scholars in a forest clearing. The ancient philosopher sits cross-legged on a rock in the midst of his attentive devotees, as he engages them in lively and engaging dialogue.[2] The subject had resonance for Rosa, who was known for gathering writers around himself for impassioned discussions.[3] AM

1   Jonathan Scott, *Salvator Rosa: His Life and Times* (New Haven and London: Yale University Press, 1995), 149-150. Rosa often got help with classical subjects from his friend Giovanni Battista Ricciardi.

2   Richard Wallace, *The Etchings of Salvator Rosa* (Princeton: Princeton University Press, 1979), 272-74; and Scott, *Salvator Rosa*, 156-157.

3   Scott, *Salvator Rosa*, 55-59, on the Academy of the Percossi held in Rosa's home in Florence, and in Volterra, and 90-91 on the recitation of his satires to audiences.

History of La Salle University Art Museum

The La Salle University Art Museum opened its doors in 1975 as an educational resource for La Salle students, especially those majoring in art history, as well as for the communities in the surrounding area. The Art Museum's collection had its beginnings 10 years earlier. At the University's fall Honors Convocation in 1965, John Walker, director of the National Gallery of Art in Washington, D.C., delivered the address, and well-known collector Lessing Rosenwald and American artist Andrew Wyeth received honorary degrees. On this auspicious occasion, the University announced that it was beginning a degree program in art history and had begun acquiring art. What began as a modest study collection has since blossomed into a well-established museum, now considered one of the city's cultural gems. Currently, La Salle is the only university in the Philadelphia area to own a permanent display of paintings, drawings, and sculptures from the Renaissance to the present. The collection is housed in a series of period rooms in the lower level of Olney Hall on the University's Main Campus.

The mission of the La Salle University Art Museum is to further the University's Lasallian educational objectives by helping students, other members of the University community, and the general public to experience significant, original works of art in an intimate setting and to place them in meaningful contexts. In addition to acquiring, preserving, and exhibiting its collections, the museum offers viewers an opportunity to sharpen their aesthetic perception and to investigate the interrelationships that emerge between art and other disciplines.

The Art Museum's comprehensive collection of European and American art features examples of major artists and historical stylistic movements in a wide range of subjects and media. Highlights from the permanent collection include Jan Provost's *Nativity*, Tintoretto's *Portrait of an Unknown Gentleman*, Thomas de Keyser's *Pendant Portraits of a Husband and Wife*, Rembrandt Peale's *Self-Portrait*, Henry Ossawa Tanner's *Mary*, George Rouault's *Last Romantic*, Edouard Vuillard's *Madame Hessel in Conversation*, Dame Elizabeth Frink's *Walking Madonna*, and Alex Katz's *Portrait of Neil Welliver*. The collections have grown through gifts from alumni, friends, La Salle University Art Museum Art Angels, and purchases.